The Art & Design Series

PB

684
STO

Stokes, Gordon

Woodturning for
pleasure

DATE			

For beginners, students, and working professionals in both fine and commercial arts, these books offer practical, how-to introductions to a variety of areas in contemporary art and design.

Each illustrated volume is written by a working artist, a specialist in his or her field, and each concentrates on an individual area—from advertising layout or printmaking to interior design, painting, and cartooning, among others. Each contains information artists will find useful in the studio, in the classroom, and in the marketplace.

Ideas for Woodturning, Anders Thorlin
Carving Wood and Stone: An Illustrated Manual, Arnold Prince
Nature Drawing: A Tool for Learning, Clare Walker Leslie
Photographic Lighting: Learning to See, Ralph Hattersley
A Practical Guide for Beginning Painters, Thomas Griffith
Transparent Watercolor: Painting Methods and Materials, Inessa Derkatsch

GORDON STOKES

Revised by ROBERT LENTO

WOODTURNING FOR PLEASURE

A SPECTRUM BOOK

Prentice-Hall Inc., Englewood Cliffs, New Jersey 07632

Library of Congress Cataloging in Publication Data

Stokes, Gordon.
    Woodturning for pleasure.

    (A Spectrum Book)
    Includes index.
    1. Turning. I. Lento, Robert, 1933-
II. Title.
TT201.S76 1980   684′.083   80-17282
ISBN 0-13-962563-1
ISBN 0-13-962555-0 (pbk.)

10 9 8 7 6 5 4 3 2 1

Printed in the United States of America

Editorial/production supervision by Frank Moorman
Interior design by Frank Moorman and Dawn Stanley
Cover design by Ira Shapiro
Art director: Jeannette Jacobs
Manufacturing buyer: Barbara A. Frick

PRENTICE-HALL INTERNATIONAL, INC., *London*
PRENTICE-HALL OF AUSTRALIA PTY. LIMITED, *Sydney*
PRENTICE-HALL OF CANADA, LTD., *Toronto*
PRENTICE-HALL OF INDIA PRIVATE LIMITED, *New Delhi*
PRENTICE-HALL OF JAPAN, INC., *Tokyo*
PRENTICE-HALL OF SOUTHEAST ASIA PTE. LTD., *Singapore*
WHITEHALL BOOKS LIMITED, *Wellington, New Zealand*

CONTENTS

Many beginners spend a great deal of time in mastering the correct techniques of tool manipulation, which were fully discussed in my earlier book, *Modern Woodturning*, only to find that they have difficulty in respect of design. The ability to cut wood properly leaving the surface with a beautiful, smooth finish is most satisfying. Unless inspiration happens to flow freely and naturally, however, there is likely to be difficulty over the question of specific shapes.

Most turners who have worked on a production basis, selling their products either through trade outlets or by retailing them among friends and acquaintances, will know that the shape which pleases the turner is not always the one to succeed—in fact things which appeal strongly to the producer often fail to impress potential buyers, and vice versa. This does not mean that any shape will do, but it is a pity to get into a rut where design is concerned. This book has been written because so many people complain that there is little guidance on the subject, but it should be borne in mind that the shapes and dimensions illustrated need not be followed exactly so long as the proportions are retained. I suggest the reader use the square grid system to enlarge the drawings which can be modified to taste and used as a starting point.

BEFORE STARTING

A beginner who has found a shape which appeals and made a drawing or template, frequently experiences difficulty in working out the best method for tackling the job. Unless the approach is correct there are likely to be quite unnecessary problems as, for instance, when gouges are used to form curves while their paths are still obstructed by wood which ought to have been removed at the outset. References to the various designs and instructions will soon make this clear.

Throughout the book, emphasis is laid on the need to cut the wood with sharp edges, properly applied, rather than the simple and inefficient use of scrapers. This is very important because the use of scrapers or scraping methods not only produces an inferior finish, but also renders the production of a finished article with crisp outlines very difficult and often impossible. Fine detail which has been scraped will need much sanding, and this will blur its outlines. In many cases examination of the work after the turning is complete will show that little pieces of wood have been knocked out, leaving jagged edges which cannot in any event be sanded smooth.

Anyone who wishes to become a woodturner should be taught by someone fully versed in the craft from whom he will acquire the basic tool technique without which true proficiency cannot be achieved.

I have private pupils coming to me from all over the world for two-day intensive courses and teach many students by correspondence. Obviously it is not possible to make anyone into a good woodturner in so short a space of time, and I do not suggest that it can be done. What is possible is to impart sufficient knowledge to enable the student to practice and so become truly proficient. I cannot teach tool control, which the student will learn independently, but if the preliminary instruction is of the right quality he will have few problems, and practice will soon improve workmanship.

There are two very important rules which must be stated and which are vital to successful work. The first is that the bevel of any tool, with the exception of a scraper, must rub firmly against the wood during the cut with the depth of cut or thickness of shaving being controlled by altering the angle of attack of the edge. The second is that with all tools,

including scrapers, only that part of the edge which is receiving direct support from the tool rest can safely be used. If these two rules are fully understood and obeyed at all times, woodturning will become a pleasure and the danger of a dig-in will be avoided.

The ability to design shapes will be of little benefit to a beginner unless he also has the ability to execute them properly, and this is really a matter of having full command of certain basic techniques.

If the tools are handled so well that the whole of the turner's attention can be devoted to the shaping of his project, life will be very easy for him. The only thing which will bring about this happy state of affairs is good basic training followed by stead and regular practice.

It is unlikely that the reader will like every design or shape in this book. Some of the designs have been included simply because they call for the use of certain cuts or a combination of cuts and are therefore very good general practice pieces. They will be of interest to many because step-by-step instructions and working notes have been provided which will help a great deal towards a successful job. These are all shapes which I have made and some are designed as exercises for my students, so the virtues and the pitfalls are well known.

Wooden tableware is often a very good selling line for those either trying to make a living or to augment their incomes by means of their hobby. Craft and gift shops are always interested in high quality items. Moreover, although demand is high, there is a notable lack of softwood items in the shops because their turning is rather difficult. It follows that proficiency in producing well-made soft-wood pieces is often a profitable sideline.

Projects or ideas which call for special equipment have been avoided as far as possible. Most of the items included are well within the scope of a newcomer to the craft who has a good quality lathe with a few accessories. Line drawings have been used as often as possible for clarification.

One very important reason for writing this book has been the fact that once someone has mastered the use of the tools, he needs designs and projects to keep from becoming nothing more than a "doodler." To put a piece of wood into a lathe and stop cutting when a pleasing shape has appeared is only a small part of the woodturner's art. To be worthy of the name it is necessary to be able to set out with a definite shape in mind and to produce that shape. If the would-be turner evades this issue, he will never be capable of satisfactory copy turning and will frequently be embarrassed when asked to repair an article of furniture or copy a favorite shape. I have given some guidelines on copy turning as such which is not popular with amateur turners because it is difficult or considered to be so.

It must be borne in mind that the shapes given in this book have been designed to be cut with really sharp tools; if the tools used are not sharp, success is unlikely. For this reason some space has been devoted to the question of correct tool sharpening, and for the real beginner, some practice with a grindstone and a few pieces of scrap metal would be an excellent idea.

Many newcomers to cutting tools of various kinds allow themselves to be misled by the idea that their sharpening is some sort of

Woodworkers' Conversion Tables

Inches	Millimeters	Millimeters	Inches
1/12	0.8	1	0.039
1/16	1.6	2	0.078
1/8	3.2	3	0.118
3/16	4.8	4	0.157
1/4	6.4	5	0.196
5/16	7.9	6	0.236
3/8	9.5	7	0.275
7/16	11.1	8	0.314
1/2	12.7	9	0.354
9/16	14.3	10	0.393
5/8	15.9	20	0.787
11/16	17.5	30	1.181
3/4	19.1	40	1.574
13/16	20.6	50	1.968
7/8	22.2	60	2.362
15/16	23.8	70	2.755
1	25.4	80	3.148
2	50.8	90	3.542
3	76.2	100	3.936
4	101.4	150	5.904
5	127.0	200	7.872
6	152.4	300	11.808
7	177.5	400	15.744
8	203.2	500	19.680
9	228.6	600	23.616
10	254.0	700	27.552
11	279.5	800	31.488
12	304.8	900	35.424
18	457.2	1,000	39.360
24	609.6		
36	914.4		

Note: The English and metric sizes given for tools and joint parts, etc., cannot work out exactly, but providing one works with one or the other, there is no difficulty. In lumbering, it is accepted that 1 inch equals 25 millimeters.

magic art. It is nothing of the sort, the requirements for success being common sense and plenty of practice.

One very important word of advice. Put away the oilstones and save them for sharpening ordinary woodworking tools. The turner uses a grindstone very frequently and an oilstone very rarely, for the edges of his tools present a different set of problems to those of the carver or cabinet-maker. One of these is frictional heat created by rubbing against the wood; remember that the edge of a turning tool can be softened or turned blue quite easily by abuse while working.

Visitors to my workshop often remark that I seem to sharpen the tools very often. Here one has to remember that a turning tool cutting wood revolving at about 2000 r.p.m. may do as much work in an hour as a carving tool or wood chisel does in months, so frequent sharpening is essential to good work.

If the tools are sharpened before starting a job and the whole project is carried out without sharpening them again, it follows that the final cuts are made with tired and dull edges. These final cuts are the only ones which will be seen in the completed workpiece, the results of the preceding ones being on the floor, so that they should always be made with edges which are at their best.

A good woodturner uses very little abrasive paper, and what he does use is medium down to fine grade. Abrasive paper, as I have said before now, is often the prop of the incompetent and it is not as helpful as many beginners seem to imagine.

I am often asked about sources of supply for various items of turning equipment such as lamp-fittings, finishing materials, nutcracker and lighter units, and so forth. I have no included any names here, because thing tend to change rapidly, but woodworking magazines carry advertisements which wil help. A list of basic tools is given on page 6 together with suggestions for a more ad vanced tool kit.

With the tools I have recommended, almos any piece of woodturning can be tackled. T have too many tools around, especially in th early stages, invites confusion. Some scrap ers will be needed, for there are times whe wood has to be scraped even though the re sulting finish will be inferior to that whicl would have come from a cutting tool. I an not, however, greatly in favor of makin scrapers from old files. The metal in these i brittle and if wrongly used may break, caus ing injury to the worker. For some odd jobs i may be necessary to make up a tool in thi way, but for the normal scraping operations good, sharp scraper made for the purpose by skilled toolmaker is infinitely preferable.

The aim in turning, if the results are good, i to take the wood off in the form of shavings s that the surface is left as smooth as possible. I the tools are merely removing dust, the worl will not be good and something is radically wrong. In this connection, the beginne should put out of his mind any idea that to be a good woodturner it is necessary to produce long shavings. This is an old-fashioned idea dating from the days when much turning was done with moist timber. Whether the shav ings are breaking up into short lengths or curling up is of no real consequence. The point is that long shavings cannot be brought off dry wood, because they shatter on leaving the tool.

Finally, a word on safety precautions. Wood-turning is a safe and relaxing occupation if correctly approached, but it can be dangerous if improper techniques are applied. For this reason I suggest that the reader adhere carefully to the instructions given in this book, deviating only under expert guidance. It is worth noting that the use of beeswax for finishing and of the grinding wheel in particular require the protection of eyeshields or goggles.

Before starting on the various projects I will run through the essential tools and some of the equipment.

Below is a set of useful tools with handles at least 304mm. (12in.) long, some of which are shown in Fig. 1-1.

Roughing gouge. 18 mm. (¾in.) half-round section, ground straight across at the end with a steep bevel.

Spindle gouges. 13mm. (½in.) and 6mm. (¼in.) ground to a fingernail shape, not to a point.

Parting tool. These are more or less standard in shape and size.

Skew chisels. 18mm. (¾in.) and 32mm. (1¼in.)

Scrapers. 25mm. to 38mm. (1in. to 1½in.) wide, one round-nosed, and one with a square end. Extreme corners of the latter are slightly rounded to avoid scoring the work.

Faceplate or bowl gouges. 6mm. (¼in.) and 9mm. (⅜in.). Ground square across the end. These are deep-fluted tools.

Dividers and calipers. Various sizes needed for marking and measuring.

Flexible rule. For ease in measuring.

Bradawl. Used mainly for marking the centers of square work and making lead holes for faceplate and woodscrew chuck screws.

Grindstone. A good one is a must, and if possible, a self-powered tool rather than a stone attached to the lathe. Whetstones are usually recommended, but they are not always available, and I have used a dry wheel over the last thirty years quite successfully. A stone of about 177mm.–203mm. (7in.–8in.) in diameter will do well, and the grit size should be about 60.

Wheel dresser. This is also essential to keep the face of the stone open. If it is not used the spaces between the abrasive grains will fill up with dust and metal fragments, the surface will become glazed, and far too much fric-

TOOLS AND EQUIPMENT

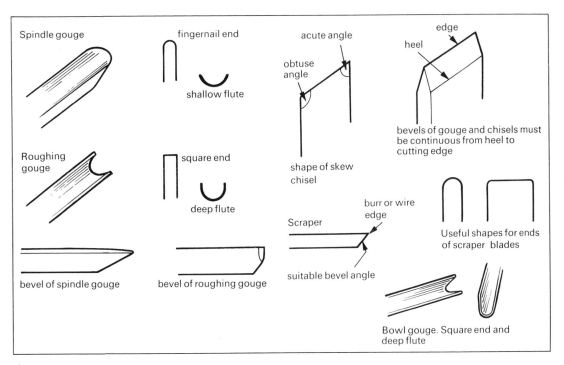

Fig. 1-1

tional heat will develop, ruining the tools. The dresser will also enable the surface of the stone to be kept flat, which is necessary for the satisfactory grinding of chisels.

Water pot. The use of one for cooling the tools as they are gound is often advocated, but unless the turner is sufficiently skilled to replace the bevel exactly where it was before the cooling process, this is not quite such a good idea as it may at first appear. I find it better to teach students to use no pressure at all when grinding, letting the tool lie against the wheel under little more than its own weight and to keep it there until they have reached the edge.

Long-hole boring kit. Items such as standard lamps or tall table lamps will need a hole drilled through them to take the wire, and there is a long-hole boring kit available for most lathes. In cases where no such kit is available, it is possible to cut the square of wood in half lengthwise before turning, groove both halves, and glue them back together so that there is a square hole running through the finished job, which will do the trick in the absence of the proper equipment.

The Basic Lathe and Auxiliary Equipment

Woodturning lathe. This is normally supplied with sufficient basic equipment to make it usable, but other items are available as extras, and these should be considered,

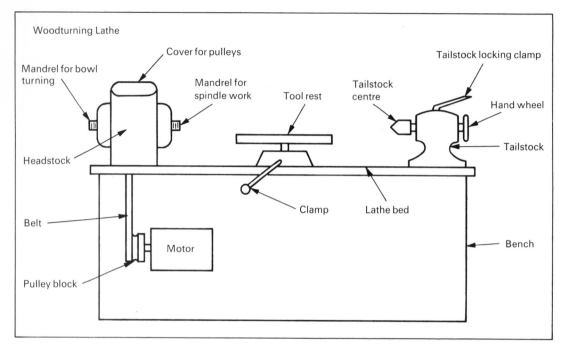

Woodturning Lathe

Cover for pulleys

Mandrel for bowl turning

Mandrel for spindle work

Tool rest

Tailstock centre

Tailstock locking clamp

Hand wheel

Tailstock

Headstock

Clamp

Lathe bed

Bench

Belt

Motor

Pulley block

Fig. 1-2

since what turns out to be essential to one person's requirements may not be so for another.

Basic equipment will probably consist of lathe with tailstock, such as that shown in Fig. 1-2, headstock, bed, and feet, plus motor with belt and pulleys. There are also one or two "saddles," and tool rest holders, a driving center of the two- or four-pronged variety, and a tailstock center. Tool rests are also part of the basic equipment, but as is pointed out, these are often so poorly designed as to be a hindrance.

Cabinet stands. Made of metal, these are available for some machines, but are often designed to give a compromise height which will suit both lathe and any attachments which may be fixed to it, such as planers and saws. The result is that the height is not cor-

rect for lengthy periods of woodturning, though it may be viable for someone who uses the lathe only on odd occasions (Fig. 1-3).

Lathe spindle. This should be positioned at a height to make it level with the elbow of the operator when standing naturally erect. If it is lower, considerable discomfort will be experienced with back pains after extended turning sessions.

Faceplates. These form part of the basic equipment, though extra ones can be useful at times, since one may wish to stop work on one job to carry on with another (Fig. 1-4). The faceplate alone is not sufficient to cope with all work, certain types of chucks being necessary (Fig. 1-5).

Woodscrew chucks. Two will be needed, one with a diameter of about 38mm. (1½in.), the other about 64mm. (2½in.), the latter having

Fig. 1-5 Section of old oak table leg in position.

Fig. 1-3 Motor of lathe positioned in cabinet stand with belt drive safely shielded.

Fig. 1-4 Lathe set up for bowl turning.

Fig. 1-6 Small jobs can be tackled successfully with a woodscrew chuck and sharp tools.

holes provided for the fitting of extra screws to give additional support. With some lathes it is not possible to obtain the smaller of these chucks, and the turner may need to have one made for him by a metal worker. These small chucks are very useful for those odd jobs like chessmen or eggcups, where it is an advantage for the chuck to have a diameter smaller than that of the work (Fig. 1-6). The size of the screw is also important, better support being given by fat screws. I never use anything smaller than a No. 14 woodscrew in these chucks. There are numerous methods of chucking work with homemade devices, and these have been dealt with as they arise.

Those chucks illustrated in the book are most useful for small work. When purchasing such a chuck, it should be checked to make sure that the center screw can easily be removed and replaced. Some chucks have screws which are brazed in position, and since these screws are easily damaged in use, this is not a good idea. Check also that the screw can be a good fat one. Thin screws are a nuisance in woodscrew chucks.

On some designs, provision is made for moving the screw in or out of the chuck, to give greater or less projection, but I never bother with this. It seems to me easier to keep some wooden discs of various thicknesses which can be slipped over the screw when necessary.

Both the 38mm. (1½in.) and 64mm. (2½in.) versions will be needed, as they are used for different types of work.

I am not necessarily suggesting that any or all of this extra equipment should be purchased immediately, but the basic kit can be added to as and when necessary, to spread the financial load.

Jacobs chucks. These have three jaws operated by a ring of teeth, as with the chuck of an electric drill. They also have a shank which is tapered to fit the taper of the headstock or tailstock, so that they can be used in either position as the occasion demands. They are used for the sort of boring which will be called for when making vases, candle holders, and the like.

A word of warning is necessary in respect of these devices. When used for drilling holes there is no danger, as the pressure involved forces the taper mounting very tight, but this is not the case when they are set up for use

with polishing wheels, sanding drums, and other accessories. Unless due care is exercised, there is a chance of their coming loose and flying from the machine, which could be extremely dangerous. If the lathe has a hollow spindle it may be possible to weld a rod to the rear of the tapered shank so that this will protrude from the other end of the spindle where it can be secured by means of washers and a wing nut. If this is not done, the taper should be set by means of a tap from a block of wood and the tailstock brought up so that it is about 1mm. (¹⁄₂₅in.) from the forward end of the object held in the chuck. This precaution will effectively prevent the chuck from coming out of the tapered spindle.

A point to watch when using these chucks, as with electric drills, is that the chuck operating key is not left in place or it may be flung out violently when the machine is started. A good dressing tool for the grinding wheels will be a worthwhile investment, and this should be used regularly, both to keep the wheels flat and square, and to maintain an open surface with sharp-edged granules which can cut properly. Failure to follow this advice will shortly produce a wheel which has almost entirely ceased to cut and is doing little more than cause excessive frictional heat.

Wheel dresser. This should be of heavy cast iron and has a number of specially shaped metal wheels or discs which are free to revolve on a spindle. Two projections on the casing of the tool are hooked over the grinding rest and, with the grinder running, the tool is pivoted until the dressing discs contact the abrasive, then the tool is moved from side to side to ensure that the face of the stone is evenly cut.

A considerable quantity of abrasive dust is produced during this process, some of it very fine, so a face mask should be worn, and of course, a good eyeshield or goggles. Cleaning and squaring-up a grinding wheel in this manner takes only a minute or so and is a very important job.

The dressing tool has two little metal flaps, one at each end of its spindle, which are held in place by screws. It is essential that frequent applications of oil be given to this spindle, or it will quickly wear out. This is done by slackening the screws and moving the flaps aside to permit the use of the oil can.

For woodturning purposes it may be found that the surface produced on the grinding wheel by this tool is a little fierce in operation, creating an unusually pronounced burr or wire edge on the tools. I overcome this by following up the dressing operation with an application of the "devil stone." This is a small rectangular block of abrasive material impregnated with industrial diamond waste, its use being a simple matter of resting it firmly on the grinding rest and pressing it against the revolving wheel for a few seconds.

The dressing tool I have described is relatively inexpensive, but diamond dressing tools can be obtained. These are more effective in skilled hands, but not suitable for the beginner. In the interests of safety some form of eye protection should always be used when the grinding wheel is in operation. The type of double-ended grinding machine produced for home or light workshop use is quite safe if treated with common sense and some understanding, but there are some factors which ought to be considered. The wheels are strong, but brittle. Sharp knocks can crack them and a wheel which has been dropped should definitely not be used unless an expert has examined it. Thick paper discs are fitted between the wheel and the retaining washers and these must not be removed. The nut which holds the wheel on the spindle must not be tightened excessively, but just sufficiently to do the job.

Speed of rotation is of vital importance, and great danger is sometimes present in home-made grinding machines in this respect. New wheels have a safe maximum r.p.m. marked on them, which must not be exceeded, or a very serious accident is possible due to the stone breaking up under the effect of centrifugal force. Soft materials like wood, plastic, and nonferrous metals must not be ground on these wheels or they will rapidly become clogged. They should be preserved for cutting steel.

Sanding discs. The woodturner finds many uses for these discs, which can be fitted to the lathe mandrel and are usually obtainable from the manufacturer. There is a case, however, for making them from blockboard discs which can be screwed to a faceplate, so that several can be kept handy with various grades of abrasive paper on them. With a little ingenuity it should also be possible to make a strong table to support the work being sanded, perhaps fixing it to the tool rest holder.

Finishing compound. Various types are mentioned and a selection of these should be kept on hand, together with a good supply of polishing cloths.

Wire for lamps can be purchased in bulk on cardboard drums which is the cheapest way to obtain it.

Lamp fittings. These should be bought in fair quantities to save expense.

I have tried as far as possible to arrange the designs in each section in order of difficulty, starting off with the easiest. In the case of table lamps, a study of shop windows or displays will reveal that many of today's designs are very simple indeed, and some are within the abilities of even a raw beginner (see Fig. 2-1 and 2-2). One thing about all design is most important and all too often overlooked, this being that it should be functional as well as attractive. A beautiful table lamp is all very well, but not if it falls over at the slightest provocation! In selecting a design to be used with a specific block of wood, or vice versa, it is as well to remember that fiddly shapes look best in plain wood, which has little distinctive grain, and that the more exotic figured woods look best with clean, simple lines.

The blocks of wood to be used for table lamps should be drilled for the wire before the turning is done. In fact my own method is to drill a few dozen blocks and keep them handy to use when required. This is quicker in the long run than setting up the machine each time just to drill one hole, but there is a more important reason. When a lamp has been turned with care and all has gone well it is very annoying to damage the finish during the drilling of the hole, and this is very easily done.

In setting about the turning of blocks which have been pre-drilled, something has obviously to be done about the hole in the center, because the job will be difficult to set up in the machine using a driving center in the normal manner. The usual answer to this problem is to use the counterbore supplied with the long-hole boring kit, which has a pin protruding from the center which will fit the hole and the fangs will drive the wood (Fig. 2-3 and 2-4). In the absence of one of these useful items it may be necessary to plug the hole at the driven end so that the ordinary diving center can be used. The hole at the other end presents no difficulties as the tailstock center can be run in it.

TABLE LAMPS

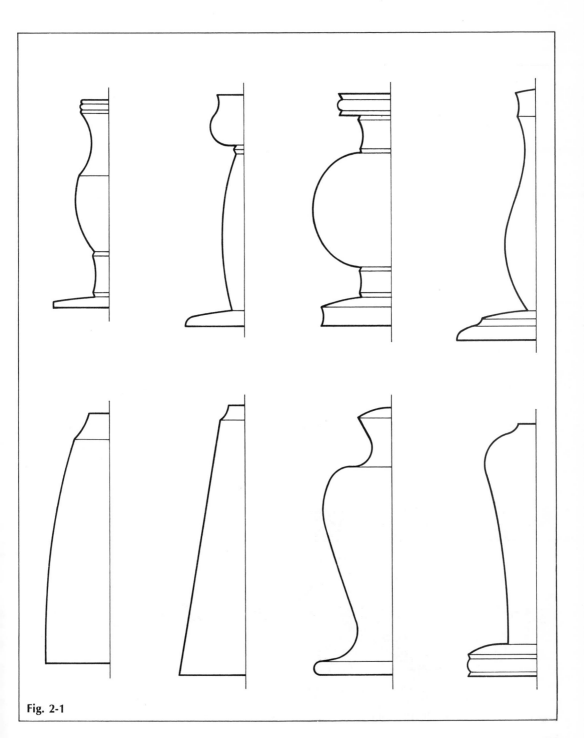

Fig. 2-1

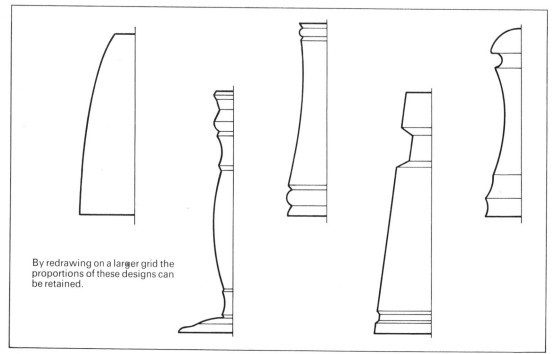

By redrawing on a larger grid the proportions of these designs can be retained.

Fig. 2-2

The design shown in Fig. 2-5A is very simple but this does not mean that it can be tackled in a careless manner. Even the simplest of shapes needs to be dealt with accurately if the finished object is to be a credit to the turner. Do not be deceived by the simple lines, for the tapered outline must be straight to be effective, and the curve at the top has to be a true

Fig. 2-3 Long-hole boring kit. Here the auger is being pushed into the revolving wood through the drilling jig mounted in a toolrest holder.

Fig. 2-4 Counterbore mounted in the headstock so job can be reversed on to it when it has been drilled a little over halfway.

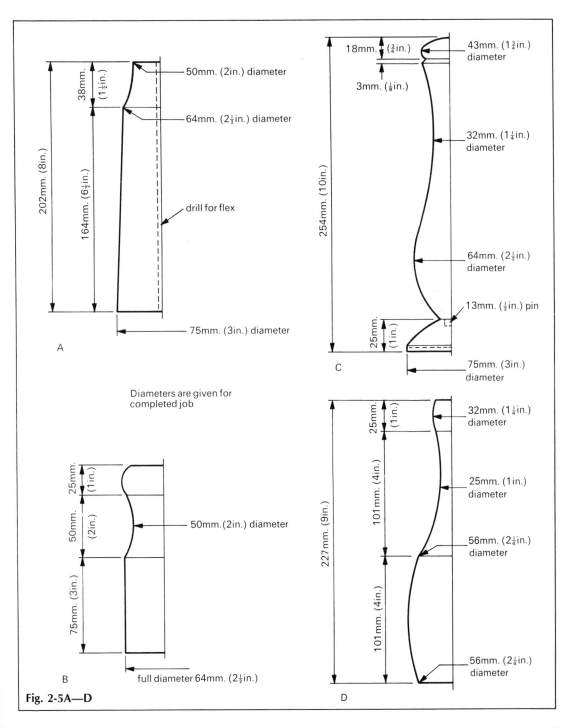

A
50mm. (2in.) diameter
64mm. (2½in.) diameter
drill for flex
75mm. (3in.) diameter
202mm. (8in.)
164mm. (6½in.)
38mm. (1½in.)

Diameters are given for completed job

B
50mm. (2in.) diameter
full diameter 64mm. (2½in.)
25mm. (1in.)
50mm. (2in.)
75mm. (3in.)

C
18mm. (¾in.)
3mm. (⅛in.)
43mm. (1¾in.) diameter
32mm. (1¼in.) diameter
64mm. (2½in.) diameter
13mm. (½in.) pin
75mm. (3in.) diameter
254mm. (10in.)
25mm. (1in.)

D
32mm. (1¼in.) diameter
25mm. (1in.) diameter
56mm. (2¼in.) diameter
56mm. (2¼in.) diameter
227mm. (9in.)
25mm. (1in.)
101mm. (4in.)
101mm. (4in.)

Fig. 2-5A—D

15

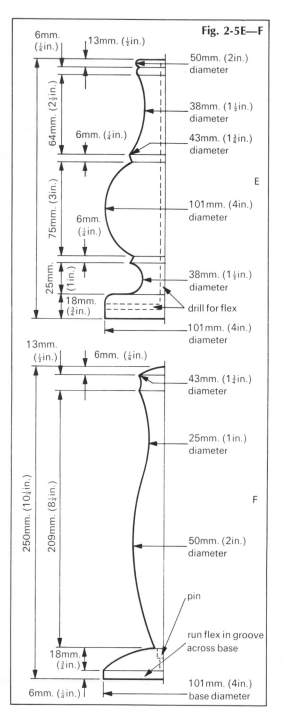

Fig. 2-5E—F

6mm. (¼in.)
13mm. (½in.)
50mm. (2in.) diameter
64mm. (2½in.)
38mm. (1½in.) diameter
6mm. (¼in.)
43mm. (1¾in.) diameter
E
75mm. (3in.)
101mm. (4in.) diameter
6mm. (¼in.)
25mm. (1in.)
38mm. (1½in.) diameter
18mm. (¾in.)
drill for flex
101mm. (4in.) diameter
13mm. (½in.)
6mm. (¼in.)
43mm. (1¾in.) diameter
25mm. (1in.) diameter
250mm. (10¾in.)
209mm. (8¼in.)
F
50mm. (2in.) diameter
pin
run flex in groove across base
18mm. (¾in.)
6mm. (¼in.)
101mm. (4in.) base diameter

curve rather than a shape made up from several curves with slight changes of direction. Sharp tools and careful cutting are imperative.

Dimensions are given in the drawings and they can be altered if desired. What I am trying to do is to provide ideas for basic shapes and some help in achieving them. Some of the instructions given for one shape will apply equally to others, so I will try to avoid repetition.

With this first lamp the opening move is to run the square block down to a cylinder with a roughing gouge (Figs. 2-6 to 2-9). This is the same with all square blocks turned between centers, unless for any reason part of the wood has to be left unturned.

Fig. 2-6 illustrates the first stage in roughing a square to a cylinder with the 18mm. (¾in.) half-round roughing gouge. The process is repeated in successive stages until the cylinder is complete.

Apart from the square, wood can also be cut or planed to octagonal shape prior to turning. In that case, the diagonals should first be drawn in to locate the center (Fig. 2-7), and a

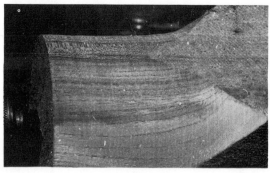

Fig. 2-6 First stage in roughing a square to a cylinder.

Fig. 2-7 If desired, wood can be planed to octagonal shape before turning.

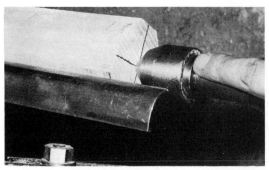

Fig. 2-9 Use of live or ball bearing center that revolves with the wood.

small hole made with a bradawl to assist in mounting in the lathe. In order to avoid strain on the lathe bearings, an old driving center is driven into the wood with a soft-faced hammer (Fig. 2-8). Fig. 2-9 shows the use of a live or ball-bearing center which revolves

with the wood. It is not really essential, but it saves the use of lubricants and the need for occasional tightening of the tailstock pressure during the turning.

Many writings on woodturning advocate the removal of the corners of such squares on a planer or circular saw, but this is quite unnecessary unless the block is too large to revolve in the lathe without striking some part of the machine (Fig. 2-10). The reason it is so often advised is that those who suggest it are not aware of the correct approach to turning a square into a cylinder and are assuming that the wood is to be scraped, but scrapers should

Fig. 2-8 Old driving center driven into the wood with a soft-faced hammer.

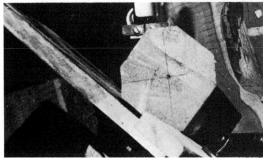

Fig. 2-10 Some beginners like to remove the corners of turning squares. Here a bandsaw is carrying out the operation, its table tilted to 45 degrees.

not be used on spindle work at all unless quite unavoidable, and this is a rare state of affairs (Fig. 2-11).

The 18mm. (¾in.) roughing gouge, freshly ground square across the end, will make a very good job of removing the corners with both speed and efficiency, but it must be used correctly for safety and good results. It is potentially dangerous to start the cutting at one end of the square and travel along to the other, for there is a chance of a dig-in at the beginning of the cut, and it is possible that one complete corner may be split away and

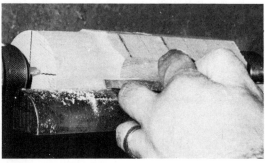

Fig. 2-11 Octagonally cut blanks can be reduced to a cylinder with a scraper, but the method is slow and inefficient.

Fig. 2-12 This photograph of a skew chisel about to commence a smoothing cut shows the problems that can arise with poorly shaped tool rests. The hard steel of the chisel causes ridges in the soft metal of the rest.

thrown up into the worker's face. The job is therefore broken up into three or more parts, taking these down to cylindrical form one at a time and at all times working so that the cut runs off the end of the wood rather than on to it (Fig. 2-12).

Make sure, also, with this or any other gouge that the bevel is presented so that it rubs the wood during the cut. I have taught several hundred people, and I think that every one of them has had a tendency to hold the handle of the tool too high, so that the tool is trying to take a heavier cut than intended. To try to remedy this situation by holding the edge back from the wood results in a scraping action, thus dulling the cutting edge in a very short time.

When the wood is cylindrical, the diameter at the upper end of the taper can be set in by making a parting tool cut, using a pair of calipers to make the resulting diameter about 2mm (¹/₁₆in.) larger than the final dimension. This should be done with all such sizing cuts to allow for final smoothing and sanding. Check the other end of the wood for diameter and correct as necessary.

The taper can now be worked in using the roughing gouge and taking the parting tool cuts as a guide. At this stage the taper is continued right through to the end. With all spindle work, that is work which is mounted between centers, the upper outline of the job should be watched in order to achieve the desired shape.

The line from top to bottom of the taper is intended to be dead straight and will look bad if it is not. To ensure this I would use a skew chisel for the final cuts, cutting downhill along the taper with a fine cut from the sharp edge. Whereas the gouge will tend to follow the humps and hollows and to reproduce them, a chisel properly used will slice off the high spots and slide over the low ones and is far more likely to produce a straight run. Remember in using this tool for smoothing that only the part of the cutting edge which is directly supported by the tool rest can be used effectively, and a little thought with the tool placed on the rest and against the wood will soon show that this will be in the third of the blade nearest to the short corner.

When the taper is to your satisfaction the length of the curved section is marked on the wood, using a pencil or the point of a skew chisel touched lightly to the wood. A spindle gouge will be used to put the curve in, and I would suggest a very sharp 13mm. (½in.) one. It will be used partly on its side and, since in this case the cut will run from left to right, the right hand side of the tool will be on the tool rest and the right hand section of the edge will do the work throughout the cut.

The job should be started near the end of the wood, taking small curving cuts and moving back a little along the work at the start of each, again watching the upper outline to see that the curve is like the one in the drawing, not like part of a cotton reel.

Remember that many of the suggestions made apply to any job. The one I wish to give now is typical; it is essential for the bevel to sit down firmly on the surface of the wood and to slide along it during the cut. If this is done, there will be a certain burnishing effect which is quite unmistakable and very satisfying. If the bevel is not properly on the wood, even though the worker thinks it is, this polished effect will not be achieved, and

there are likely to be unsightly little ridged lines on the surface instead.

Another helpful point is that in a concave curve, the handle will be moving backwards, whereas in a convex curve it will be moving forwards. Try this on the inside and outside of an enamel bowl or something of the kind, and my meaning will quickly become apparent to you.

When the curve has been dealt with, the right hand end of the job will need attention. It will presumably have a sawn surface, and this should not be left in the hope that abrasive paper will smooth it afterwards, for that is unlikely to work. The long corner of a skew chisel is used to trim this surface, but only the actual point of the tool touches the wood. If more than the point is allowed to touch there will be a spectacular dig-in; in fact, the rest of the blade is leaning very slightly away from the wood as the point goes forward. Some turners would be satisfied with a parting tool cut to trim this end grain, but I do not find the finish produced good enough.

If the tool work has been up to standard, the job should now be finished as far as turning goes, but the lathe should be stopped and the surface thoroughly examined before using any abrasive paper. If any flaws are evident, these must be corrected with sharp tools, not left in the hope that they will sand out.

If abrasive paper is required, and it may be, this should be folded to avoid burning the fingers and always used underneath the job rather than on top. This avoids having fingers bent back, throws most of the dust away from the worker, and allows him to see what he is doing. The abrasive paper used in lathe work is not sandpaper, but garnet, which is

19

orange-red in color. It is expensive, but good turners use very little, and it will stand up to the job well. It is possible to buy either open or closed coat, the former having less granules per square centimeter, but the latter tends to clog too quickly when used in woodturning. Finishing methods are dealt with on page 106, but for a table lamp I normally use either a friction polish or one of the waxes.

If the lamp is now removed from the machine, a hole can be drilled across the grain, about 13mm. (½in.) from the bottom, to meet the center hole and permit the fitting of the wire.

It will not be necessary to describe in full detail the turning of each individual shape, since much of the work will be the same. It will be noted that the design in Fig. 2-5B is rather similar to Fig. 2-5A with a straight and a curved section, but there is also a curve at the top which will need to be cut carefully. The job is mounted in the lathe and brought to a cylinder as before, then the lengths of the straight and curved section are marked in, leaving the extreme top to be dealt with last.

In order to arrive at the curved neck the 13mm. (½in.) spindle gouge is used, starting at the center of the area which is to be cut with alternate cuts from left and right, widening and deepening the neck steadily and ensuring that the bevel is rubbing.

Note that, where possible, all cuts in woodturning are made downhill, or from a large diameter to a smaller one. This is important, and if the advice is ignored there will certainly be some dig-ins. Watch the upper outline and when the cut is nearly deep enough begin checking for size with the calipers.

The straight section will now need some treatment. Use a sharp skew to make one or two light smoothing cuts along the surface, having first established that the diameter is correct. Bear in mind that the object in using this tool is not to remove vast quantities of wood or to produce bigger and better shavings. What is needed is a fine, light cut which will give the best possible surface finish. The curve at the top end can now be put in with the spindle gouge. Take care to cut with the correct part of the edge, swinging the handle round rapidly to keep the bevel rubbing all the time. If this is done properly, the finish produced will resemble a billiard ball.

A final cut with the chisel point across the end grain will complete the turning. Remember that in this cut the tool can only take the thickness of a shaving in one pass; any attempt to take a heavy cut will result in a burned and softened chisel point.

After sanding this sort of job, it may be found helpful to burnish the surface with a handful of *soft* shavings, care must be taken that hard shavings are not picked up by accident for these will score rings around the wood.

The shape of the lamp in Fig. 2-5C is deceptively simple, and the beginner will soon realize that slow curves are far more difficult to get exactly right than rapid ones. The answer here is simply continuous practice. This project is not the same as the preceding ones, because the lamp is made in two parts. Many table lamps are made this way so that the base can be wide enough to give stability, while the stem is made from a relatively thin piece of wood to save wastage. The two are eventually joined by means of a pin at the end of the stem which is glued into a hole in the base.

In this design, however, we have an example of a shape which does not lend itself to being drilled through from the side to take the wire, and an alternative method must be used. It would be possible to take the wire in above the base where it meets the stem, but this does not look particularly neat. A better idea is to cut a groove with a sharp wood chisel across the underside of the base to the center hole and to fix the wire firmly into this with a high-strength adhesive. This prevents the self-adhesive green baize which is applied as a finishing touch from being ripped away if the wire is pulled sharply at any time.

The stem can be made first, the wood being run down to a cylinder a little larger than the required diameter and a pin cut with the parting tool at the left hand end (Fig. 2-13). Once this has been done the shaping of this end can begin, working carefully with a sharp spindle gouge, bevel rubbing firmly. Get this end roughed to shape but not completed, then begin work on the remaining section, starting at about the middle of the area which is to form the hollow and working alternately

Fig. 2-13 Parting tool cut across cylinder end. This produces a fairly rough finish, but is a quick way to square up an end. The cut should be at ten o'clock on the circle throughout.

from each side until the concave shape is nearly wide and deep enough. The lamp will now be roughly the right shape, and the gouge can be sharpened up for the finishing cuts. The top part is left until last, ignoring the little shoulder, which is put in as a final touch with the corner of a skew chisel. Give the job a final critical inspection to make quite sure that the lines are right, then it can be sanded. Be careful of the little shoulder at the top which should have a crisp sharp edge which will be lost if too much sanding is done on it.

A disc of wood for the base is mounted on a large woodscrew chuck, using the center screw only as there is no real need for the two additional ones. In a lot of faceplate and chuck work, the retaining screw or screws will be in end grain, but in this case the grain is across the job and the screw will hold well.

Set up the tool rest about 3mm. (⅛in.) from the edge of the disc, and with a deep-fluted bowl gouge, trim the edge straight bringing the wood down almost to the required diameter. These gouges are used slightly on their sides, always moving in the direction of the flute, and they cut extremely well if properly ground.

The tool rest is now moved around to the front of the job and, if necessary, a preliminary cut can be made from the center to the edge to clean up the work. The exact size of the hole required to accommodate the pin on the stem can now be marked, and for this I use a Vernier pattern caliper, setting it to the pin and transferring the measurement to the revolving wood by pressing the points against it carefully. The hole is cut with a parting tool, taking the edge in to the depth needed in one pass, then repeating this process until only a small piece of wood is left at the center. This is not cut away, but broken out when the job is finished, otherwise the parting tool and the retaining screw may meet.

The next process is the shaping of the curved base, which in this instance is a fairly straightforward job. The deep-fluted 9mm. (⅜in.) gouge will be best, but those less confident may be able to get away with the use of a scraper, provided it is really sharp. When the curve is satisfactory, the edge can be given a final trim to bring it to the exact diameter and, after final sanding, the job can be taken off the chuck and the central pin of wood broken away.

Lamps as shown in Fig. 2-5D and E are fairly large, and it will be noted that Fig. 2-5D has a strong similarity to Fig. 2-5B apart from its size, so the methods of operation will be somewhat alike. Where a fair quantity of wood has to be removed to make a concave curve, the roughing gouge can be used to get most of it out of the way, finishing off with a spindle gouge in the normal manner. Fig. 2-5E poses certain problems which have not occurred in the others, not the least of which being that the central portion is part of a ball, and the turner will find that this shape is one of the most difficult to cut by freehand methods. There is also the fact that the three little shoulders should be exactly the same width and diameter, so care should be exercised in cutting them.

In the turning of Fig. 2-5F one of the most difficult problems of freehand woodturning may well arise. This is ribbing, the formation of spiral markings on the wood during the cutting. It occurs when a workpiece is thin in relation to its length, and I am frequently asked about it. What happens is that the pressure of the tool causes the wood to bend slightly and it tries to climb up on to the cutting edge. The answer most commonly given is that a steady should be used to support the work, this being a metal device obtainable from most manufacturers for their particular lathes. Certainly this will help, although there are disadvantages in that a steady always seems to be in the way of the cut and it tends to mark the wood.

I use the old system adopted by professional turners who were working on piece-work rates and had no time to spare, which is to support the wood by putting the left hand round it, using the tool with the right. Slight pressure from the left hand counteracts that of the tool and with care the trouble can be overcome, though if too much pressure is applied, the hand may become a trifle warm!

Fig. 2-14–16 show the different finishes obtained using scraper and gouge. Fig. 2-14 illustrates a poor finish produced by the scraper with a tell-tale accumulation of dust on the tool rest. Fig. 2-15 shows how a blunt gouge no longer produces clean shavings.

Fig. 2-14 Shape formed with scraper.

Fig. 2-15 A gouge which has lost its cutting edge no longer produces clean shavings.

Fig. 2-16 Rough shaping with a 13mm. (½in.) gouge.

The presence of dust is indicative of the need for sharpening. The final photograph shows a satisfactory finish. Here rough shaping is done with the 13mm. (½in.) gouge and the smooth surface achieved without abrasive work.

CANDLE HOLDERS

The term "candlestick" seems to have died out in recent years and "candle holder" is a better description of the more squat type now in vogue. The making of candles, though messy, is far from difficult, and since the introduction of home candlemaking kits, it has become very popular. This is a good thing for the turner who can profit by turning up holders for all types, even producing his own candles to go with his holders.

One important point should be mentioned at the start. While it is desirable that table lamps stand firmly on their bases, it is essential that this is so in the case of candle holders. Remember too that the top of a candle holder should be dished to allow the excess wax to collect around the base of the candle.

Most candle holders are bored out, or excavated with a parting tool to take the candle, and this is not difficult. An alternative which can sometimes be used to good effect involves fitting a brass spike in the top of the holder which can be warmed and the candle pushed on to it. The spike can be turned up in a lathe from a piece of brass rod and here a lathe that accepts metal turning accessories can be useful. If preferred, a large brass screw can be used with the thread filed off.

If such a spike is to be fitted, the best method will be to drill the hole for it in the top of the holder by using a drill mounted in the tailstock, feeding this into the revolving wood. The result will be a truly central hole, whereas if drilling is done after the job has been turned and removed from the lathe it will frequently be found to have gone off center, owing to the drill wandering in the grain.

Candle holders are items frequently called for in pairs or sets, which involves copy turning. I have discussed the finer points of this later in the book, as it is a constant source of questions, but for the moment I will deal with the individual shapes shown in the diagrams.

It is debatable whether A or B of Fig. 3-1 is the more difficult, but the former has a fitted spike to be incorporated. Having cut the wood to length with square ends, the first operation will be to mark the centers at each end by drawing in the diagonals and to make a small hole at the intersections with a bradawl. A drill is now mounted in a Jacobs chuck in the headstock and the wood is fed to this by means of the tailstock handwheel until the hole is the correct depth. When this has been done, the wood can be mounted between centers in the usual way, with the drilled end against the tailstock center. This ensures that when the spike is subsequently fitted it is truly central.

The block is now run down to a cylinder with a diameter fractionally larger than the required base size, then tapered with a gouge until the right hand end is just a little larger than required for the finished top. The section of wood which will form the top is now marked off, together with the area for the cove near the base. The cove is cut with a 13mm. (½in.) spindle gouge, making sure that it is slicing away shavings, not held so that its edge scrapes. The same gouge used on its side will trim up the foot, leaving it smooth.

The top can be shaped by rolling the point of a skew in alternately from each side, creating a sort of V-shaped channel. This will allow the top itself to be correctly shaped, and the gap which is left will mean that a gouge can be used to shape the tapering curve without running into the top section. The final part of the cutting consists of trimming the end grain at the top with a very sharp skew chisel point, as described on page 20. Sanding and the

application of the chosen finish follow in the normal way. The candle holder can then be taken from the machine and the prepared spike fitted with the aid of some strong glue.

Bear in mind that articles like this must stand without rocking so the base needs to be very slightly undercut. This can be done as part of the turning, using a sharp parting tool, stopping the cut before it reaches the driving center. The rough section which is left can be removed later on the end of a belt sander or with a sharp wood chisel, and green baize can be applied to finish the job off.

Fig. 3-1B is a small candle holder and will be turned best on the larger of the woodscrew chucks, using the extra screws. Mount the block, turn it down nearly to a cylinder but not quite, then cut across the face with a parting tool to make it very slightly concave. A sharp skew chisel point can now trim the end grain to a really smooth finish. With the tool rest across the face of the work, a bradawl can be held on it at about 45° to the front of the rest to locate the center. When this has been established, the point of the tool can be pushed into the wood a short distance and withdrawn. The job can now be removed from the chuck and reversed so that the prepared face is against the chuck. This gives edge contact all round the chuck face and means that the job will stand firmly when it is finished.

The wood is now brought to a cylindrical form with the roughing gouge, just oversize, and the bottom of the neck is marked. The curved neck is cut with the 13mm (½in.) spindle gouge, the top section being formed with a chisel point in the manner of cutting a bead. The curvature of the bottom section, which in fact is very slight, is formed with a gouge, and those with plenty of confidence

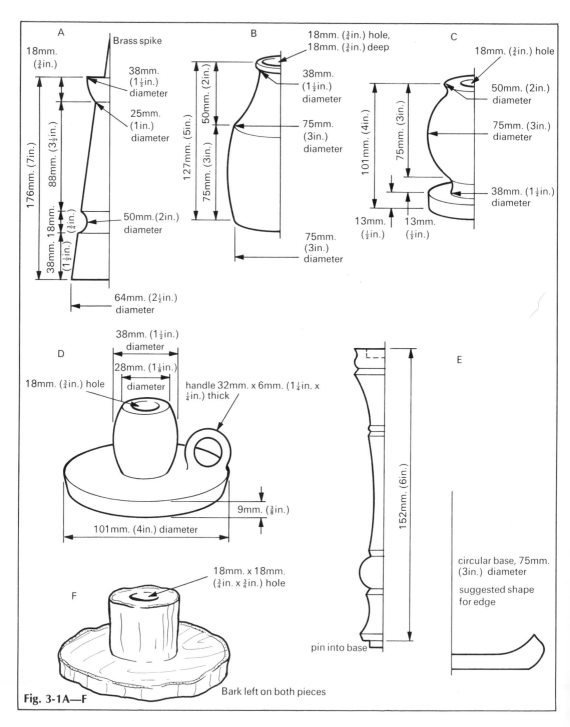

A

18mm. (¾in.)

Brass spike

38mm. (1½in.) diameter

25mm. (1in.) diameter

176mm. (7in.)

88mm. (3½in.)

38mm. 18mm. (1½in.) (¾in.)

50mm. (2in.) diameter

64mm. (2½in.) diameter

B

18mm. (¾in.) hole, 18mm. (¾in.) deep

38mm. (1½in.) diameter

127mm. (5in.)

50mm. (2in.)

75mm. (3in.)

75mm. (3in.) diameter

75mm. (3in.) diameter

C

18mm. (¾in.) hole

50mm. (2in.) diameter

101mm. (4in.)

75mm. (3in.)

75mm. (3in.) diameter

38mm. (1½in.) diameter

13mm. (½in.)   13mm. (½in.)

D

18mm. (¾in.) hole

38mm. (1½in.) diameter

28mm. (1⅛in.) diameter

handle 32mm. x 6mm. (1¼in. x ¼in.) thick

9mm. (⅜in.)

101mm. (4in.) diameter

E

152mm. (6in.)

circular base, 75mm. (3in.) diameter

suggested shape for edge

F

18mm. x 18mm. (¾in. x ¾in.) hole

pin into base

Bark left on both pieces

Fig. 3-1A—F

may like to try a final smoothing cut with a really sharp skew.

Note that, as with most of the designs given in this book, it is the proportions which are important, rather than the exact sizes; shapes can be made slightly larger or smaller if desired, but the proportions should remain the same.

Fig. 3-1C can be made equally well from one piece of wood, which is the method I used, or in two pieces, the base being a simple turned disc done on a woodscrew chuck in the manner described in chapter 2. The top section will in any event be turned on the large woodscrew chuck, and the hole is for a modern fat candle, so it is likely that the worker will not have available a suitable drill. This does not matter as the parting tool will do the job well. Mark out the size of the hole with a pencil as the work revolves, then hollow with the parting tool which must be sharp.

Start at the outer edge of the hole, going in about 25mm. (1in.), then work across the face, one cut at a time, until the hole is completed. The resulting excavation can be trimmed to exact depth quite easily. Make sure when doing this sort of operation that the parting tool is taken straight in, not at an angle, or the hole will end up with a taper which is not required.

It will be seen that the shape is basically a ball with a small cove attached at each end. As I remarked before, the ball shape is not easy and plenty of practice on scrap wood is the only way to acquire the necessary skill to cut it accurately. The 13mm. (½in.) gouge is used for the whole shape with the exception of the base, this being cut with a sharp skew point using the same technique as when trimming

the end grain of a cylinder. Whatever else happens, do not attempt to use scrapers or scraping methods on any of these shapes. They can be produced this way, but the surface will be torn about and valuable time will be wasted in trying to rectify a situation which should never have arisen.

Fig. 3-1D is all woodscrew chuck work and very popular. They look very good made from a nice piece of yew, and little imagination will be required to vary the shape, should this be desired.

The holder itself is very similar to that in Fig. 3-1C, but without the coves at top and bottom. It can be made on the woodscrew chuck, leaving some spare wood at the left-hand end so that the holder can be cut off with a parting tool after sanding. Use the tool in the right hand, catching the holder with the left as it comes away. The base section is a disc, trimmed up with a deep-fluted faceplate gouge and hollowed with the same tool, though anyone who really must scrape might get away with it here if the scraper is correctly sharpened. To those who are in the habit of using scrapers on work between centers, I can only say that there is much to learn and the sooner this learning is undertaken the faster will real satisfaction be obtained from the craft.

The handle is best made by putting a small piece of wood on the woodscrew chuck, running it to a cylinder of appropriate size, shaping and polishing the outside of the ring, hollowing with the parting tool deeper than the required width of the handle, and then parting the ring off from the waste. Smoothing up of this ring can be best done by mounting another piece of scrap wood on the chuck and hollowing it with the parting tool to accept the ring as a push fit, about one third of the ring going into the homemake chuck. This method is useful for trimming all sorts of little odds and ends.

Fig. 3-1E is a two-part design, the base being formed by methods already described. The stem, however, is a fairly advanced piece of spindle turning, if it is done correctly, and will repay careful work. The wood for this should be prepared a little oversize to allow for a pin to be left on the bottom to engage with a hole in the base. Note that the hole to take the candle must be drilled before any turning is done. If the wood is held firmly and the lathe speed is kept low, there is no real danger.

The first stage is to bring the wood to a cylinder which has a diameter a fraction greater than the largest diameter of the finished job; the extra wood allows for the final smoothing and sanding. It now needs to be marked out where the alterations in contour occur and I normally use a chisel point for this because a pencil is too easily mislaid in the shavings. Bear in mind that the point of the chisel cannot be pushed deeply into the wood without burning it, which is obviously undesirable, so the marking must be done lightly. At this stage there is no real benefit in marking out more than the detail at the right hand end as the diameter has soon to be decreased along the work and this will obliterate the marks anyway.

The work on the top part of the turning is done with a gouge for the cove and a chisel point to cut the remainder of the detail. When this has been done the roughing gouge can be used to start from the right-hand side of the completed detail, going in a curve down to the maximum diameter of the rest of the turn-ing. The neck at the right-hand side is now formed with a 13mm. (½in.) gouge, and a small bead is cut with the chisel point. The ball shape near the other end is also best made with the corner of a chisel, as this will cut cleanly and do a neat job.

When cutting the original block of wood for the making of the stem, remember that candle holders which need to have holes drilled should have this done before turning commences. Use an appropriate size drill bit in a chuck in the headstock, feeding the wood to it with the tailstock and holding the work by hand so that it cannot revolve. I am often asked if this is dangerous; with a sharp cutter revolving at the correct speed it is not, but the cutter *must* be sharp. It is also worth remembering that the speed has to be suitably reduced when using large cutters, or the friction will heat them up and soften the metal. Cutters of this type are very expensive now, so this advice should be followed. It is not really safe to use the flat bit, or spade bit, for this sort of work—at least not in the case of an inexperienced worker. These call for quite high speeds and a snatch could injure the hand. Cheap versions of this type of cutter should be avoided and certainly they should be kept well away from powerful machines. They are quite likely to bend or break and either could be dangerous.

The candle holder in Fig. 3-1F is an oddity but can look very attractive, especially on festive occasions when used as a table decoration. It is made from wood which still has its bark, and it is necessary to ensure that this is adhering firmly as a good piece of work can be spoiled if part of the bark falls away later. Yew is a good choice of timber for the project, though other woods could be used. The sec-

28

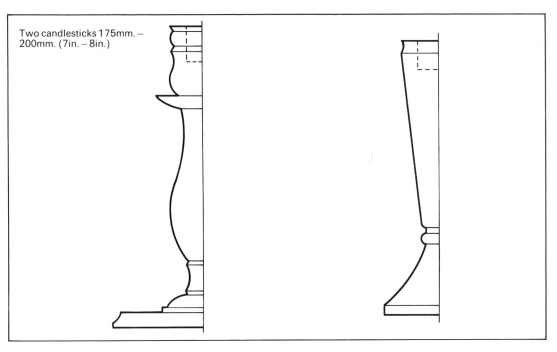

Two candlesticks 175mm. – 200mm. (7in. – 8in.)

Fig. 3-2

tion which holds the candle is cut at a slight angle so that it leans on its base. If the latter method is adopted, of course, turning hardly comes into it at all, but if the square cut is used, the wood can be mounted on a screw chuck, hollowed with the parting tool to take the candle, and dished at the top to form a wax trap. The base is sanded thoroughly on a belt sander with a fine belt and the whole

project is given a couple of coats of polyurethane after assembly.

Two further designs for candlesticks are shown in Fig. 3-2. As with all designs given, remember that so long as proportions are maintained, exact measurements depend on individual wishes. Mistakes will soon be obvious if balance is not achieved.

I enjoy making vases, perhaps because they come from small pieces of wood or because the wooden vase is so unusual. The insides of most vases will need to be scraped, because the interior is deep in relation to the width and it is not possible to keep the bevel of a gouge rubbing the wood during the cut. In using a scraper on this sort of work, however, the cutting is being done on end grain. If the tool is properly ground, there will be a shaving leaving the edge and not little pieces of dust which would indicate an inefficient and ineffective cut. Despite the fact that a scraping technique is used, care is required to achieve the desired shape without tearing the surface of the wood. Scraping is much slower than cutting, and this is something one just has to accept.

Wooden vases must be waterproofed or given some sort of lining, but this is no real problem. An old method which is often advised and which works well enough is the use of candle wax. This has to be molten and poured into the vase, but it should be removed before it has time to set, as its removal after setting is difficult. The melting of candle wax can be dangerous unless it is done with care; direct melting over gas or on an electric stove could cause a fire. The safe way is to melt it in a container which floats in boiling water, like a double boiler. The hot wax goes into the wood, impregnating it thoroughly, and the result is a waterproof interior. Another approach is to use a two-part resin plastic coating or several coats of polyurethane. Alternatively a liner must be fitted to the vase.

Rather than turn an inside shape and then try to find something to fit, it is better to use a cheap glass tumbler of suitable shape, making the inside shape able to accept it. Remember that these should not be a snug fit, there must be some room left for shrinkage of the wood likely to take place in the warmth of the home.

VASES

In chapter 5, a vase is included, and it will be noted that many shapes can be made on this built-up method. It is not true coopering, but it is the turner's equivalent and most useful. Some of the other forms of built-up work will also lend themselves to vase-making, and no book could possibly give every permutation of technique. The object is to get the beginner thinking along the right lines. The vases shown here are all from the solid, not built-up, and the choice of timber is a matter for the individual. Most woods will do reasonably well for this. The great majority of my own turning nowadays is done in home-grown timbers which are very attractive. It is extremely difficult to obtain good imported timbers, and the prices are often prohibitive.

There is one thing common to the making of all the vases illustrated: they have to be hollowed, which should be done before the outside is turned. The block is cut to size, marked (Fig. 4-1), and mounted on the larger of the woodscrew chucks with the two extra screws, and the lathe is set to run at about 500 r.p.m. With a large multi-spur bit mounted in a Jacobs chuck in the tailstock, a hole is bored to a little less than the required depth (Fig. 4-2). It is necessary to have reasonable tension on the drive belt of the machine for this operation or it will slip. This is one of those jobs where it pays to have an hour or two for preparing blocks for future use, as once the machine is set up for the job and the blocks have been cut to size, a large number can be bored quite quickly. Setting up the machine to bore just one is a waste of time.

When the boring has been done, the tool rest is swung round across the mouth of the hole, and a sharp scraper is used with light cuts to open out the aperture and bring it to the desired shape (Fig. 4-3). This part of the job

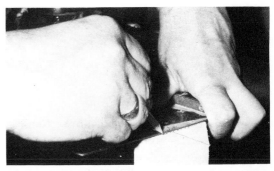

Fig. 4-1 Block for vase marked to locate center. Saw the ends of such blocks square.

Fig. 4-2 With block mounted on woodscrew chuck, a multi-spur bit is used in a chuck in the tailstock to open out the vase.

Fig. 4-3 The inside of the vase is shaped by light cuts from a scraper. Work which has been scraped will always need a fair amount of sanding.

should not be hurried. Scrapers are not the best of tools, and if they are pushed, the inevitable damage to the wood will take some time and trouble to repair. It is in fact quicker to work more slowly in such cases, sharpening the scraper whenever necessary.

When the inside of the vase is judged to have been sufficiently hollowed, remove the tool rest and, with the work stationary, feel the inside curve with the fingertips to see that there are no pronounced ridges or troughs. If all is well, the inside can be sanded. Caution is necessary according to the shape and width of the interior and, in some cases, it may be best to wrap abrasive paper round a shaped piece of wood and use this, rather than put hand or fingers into too small an orifice.

Once the inside is finished, the work can be supported by the tailstock while the outside is being dealt with (Fig. 4-4). To do this, it will be necessary to turn up a wooden plug with a slight taper; a piece of softwood will do, mounted on a woodscrew chuck. These tapered plugs should be kept for future use. With the plug fitted into the end of the vase block (Fig. 4-5), the tailstock is brought up to give just a light pressure which will be sufficient to keep the work quite steady. Be careful not to apply too much pressure; this is a common error and can result in a breakage of the wall when turned fairly thin. The roughing gouge is used in the usual way to get rid of the corners of the block, and the shaping is finished with spindle gouge and skew chisel.

When making vases, it is as well to check carefully for the exact location of the bottom of the interior when shaping the outside (Fig. 4-6). Failure to do this may well result in the job being cut in two, which has happened to

Fig. 4-4 The interior finished, the outside can be brought to a cylinder with a roughing gouge, final shaping being done with skew chisel or 13mm. (½in.) spindle gouge.

Fig. 4-5 Additional support can be given by fitting a plug and bringing up the tailstock.

Fig. 4-6 Finished project being parted off from the waste wood.

me once or twice when I have guessed instead of measured!

The vase in Fig. 4-7A is shaped like a flower pot and is a very popular design which will not present many problems. It is a very simple shape, being a taper with a bead at the upper edge. The point at which the curvature of the bead meets the straight part of the job may require a very light scrape with a sharp edge because the taper runs uphill to the bead. However, a skilled worker will be able to use a sharp skew with a smoothing action to finish this detail.

Fig. 4-7B is a little more difficult. It will be found that the slow curvature of the outside needs to be shaped with the greatest care if it is to look right. It should balance equally from the center to the ends, and this can be achieved by watching the upper outline carefully. Needless to say, the cure should be true—any slight change of direction will make it look wrong. I use a skew chisel for this sort of cut if the wood will allow, but some timbers, such as ash, reject the action of the skew edge, and small pieces may flick out of the grain. If this occurs, it is best to revert to the spindle gouge.

The stem is a straightforward cove, a real copybook cut, done with a 13mm. (½in). spindle gouge, starting with light cuts at the center of the area, working gradually deeper and wider. This curve must balance and be free of ridges or hollows.

Fig. 4-7C is in the style of a sherry glass. Here the curvature of the body is concave, so the gouge will be the best tool. To be effective, the walls will need to be thin, which calls for careful work with sharp edges. The stem is a cove with half a bead at each end, these being cut with the long corner of the skew. The surface of the base is end grain so this should be trimmed off with one continuous cut from a chisel point.

The design in Fig. 4-7D makes a nice vase but could equally well be a spill holder; if well made, it is an ornament in its own right. The turning will follow the lines of the body section in Fig. 4-7B but the bottom of the interior ought to be flat. When the outside has been turned and while the tailstock support is still available, a file tang is pushed down between the work and the tool rest and levered against the revolving wood to make neat, black friction burns, thus heightening the barrel effect.

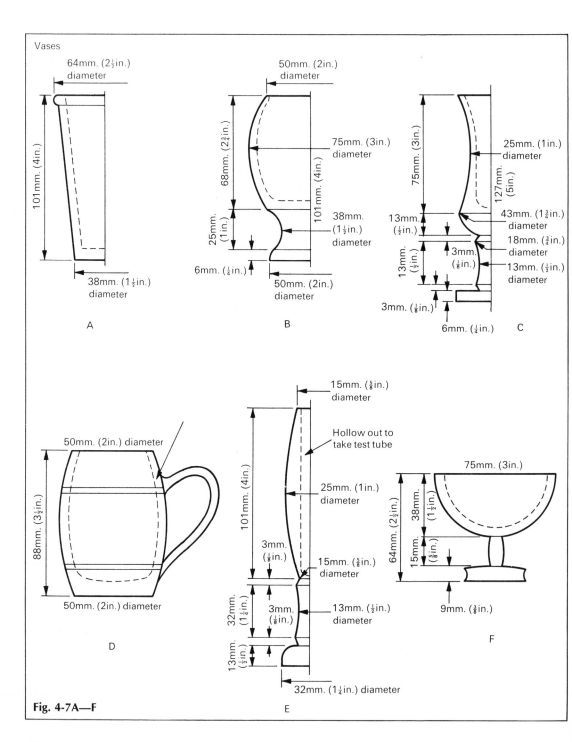

Vases

64mm. (2½in.)
diameter

101mm. (4in.)

38mm. (1½in.)
diameter

A

50mm. (2in.)
diameter

68mm. (2¾in.)

75mm. (3in.)
diameter

101mm. (4in.)

38mm.
(1½in.)
diameter

25mm.
(1in.)

6mm. (¼in.)

50mm. (2in.)
diameter

B

75mm. (3in.)

25mm. (1in.)
diameter

127mm.
(5in.)

13mm.
(½in.)

43mm. (1¾in.)
diameter

18mm. (¾in.)
diameter

13mm.
(½in.)

3mm.
(⅛in.)

13mm. (½in.)
diameter

3mm. (⅛in.)

6mm. (¼in.)

C

50mm. (2in.) diameter

88mm. (3½in.)

50mm. (2in.) diameter

D

15mm. (⅝in.)
diameter

Hollow out to
take test tube

101mm. (4in.)

25mm. (1in.)
diameter

3mm.
(⅛in.)

15mm. (⅝in.)
diameter

32mm.
(1¼in.)

3mm.
(⅛in.)

13mm. (½in.)
diameter

13mm.
(½in.)

32mm. (1¼in.) diameter

E

75mm. (3in.)

64mm. (2½in.)

38mm.
(1½in.)

15mm.
(⅝in.)

9mm. (⅜in.)

F

Fig. 4-7A—F

34

The handle is cut out with a fret saw—the exact shape is not important—and after suitable shaping and sanding, it can be attached to the vase with a strong glue.

The rose vase in Fig. 4-7E is intended to take a single rosebud and makes use of a test tube as a liner. This is not really a difficult project but it can be very effective. One special use for this sort of design is the turning of the little vase from pine which is then scorched with a naked flame, like that from a butane torch. This darkens the harder parts of the grain, and the effect is quite striking, especially

after varnishing. In making this sort of vase, a hole is drilled in the square block to a sufficient depth to accommodate a test tube; if a slightly larger shallow hole is drilled first, the lip of the tube will be hidden. Obviously, once the support plug has been inserted, care must be taken to see that the shaping of the outside does not cut through to the hole at the center. These small items are unusual, fun to make, and particularly popular. Dice shakers can also be made using the same principles described in this chapter; Fig. 4-8 and 4-9 show a variety of designs to give inspiration to the turner.

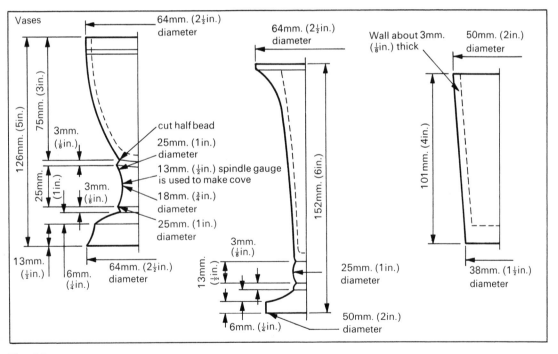

Fig. 4-8

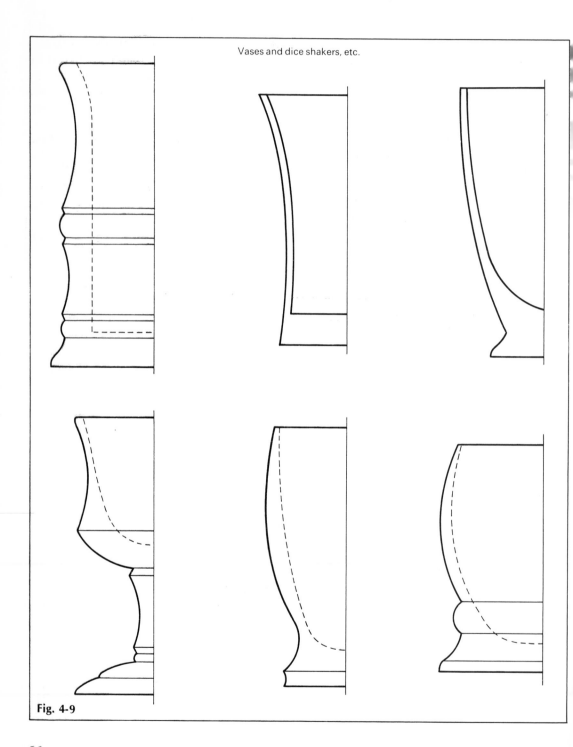

Vases and dice shakers, etc.

Fig. 4-9

This is really a misnomer because the sort of buildup I will describe is not strictly coopering at all, but this is its normal description among turners. Basically it is a method of building up hollow blanks from strip material to which bases can be fitted for turning quite a range of different articles. The staves in Fig. 5-1 could have been cut with the blade

Fig. 5-1 Batch of staves for tankard blank construction ripped to size on De Walt radial arm saw. Note wooden planing template.

COOPERED WORK

tilted to produce the required angle, but the sawn surface would not normally be as smooth as that obtained from a jointer. Alternatively, such articles as tankards would have to be hollowed out from the solid, with considerable waste of wood and consumption of time. It is often said that too much time is needed to make up such blanks, but I disagree. If a quantity of blanks is made up over a one- or two-day period, a surprising number can be produced, and the time saved in hollowing certainly offsets that spent on the buildup.

For most of my work I use eight sides in the blanks, but this can be varied as desired. I use a small jointer to cut the angles on the staves (Fig. 5-2), arriving at the figure required by dividing the number of sides in the buildup into 180° and deducting the result from 90°. With eight sides, therefore, we get 22½° which, when deducted from 90°, brings us to a figure of 67½°. A plywood or metal template is cut to give this exact angle, and placed on

Fig. 5-2 Staves after planing, ready for assembly. There is no need for further treatment of the surface prior to gluing.

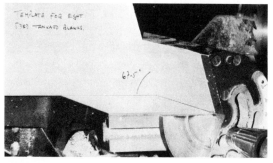

Fig. 5-3 When the fence has been set to the angle needed, it should be positioned to leave enough space for the staves to be planed without unnecessary exposure of blade, which could lead to accidents.

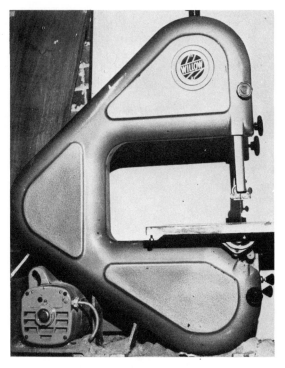

Fig. 5-4 The bandsaw shown here has a 380mm. (15in.) throat, or distance from blade to vertical part of casing. A good bandsaw is a tremendous asset to the woodturner.

the planer table to act as an accurate guide for setting the tilt of the fence (Fig. 5-3). Attempting to use the somewhat primitive tilt-setting scales which are provided will almost inevitably result in total failure.

For convenience, the blanks can be made up initially in cylinders 457mm. (18in.) or so in length, cut to suitable sizes as required on a bandsaw, (Fig. 5-4). The serious woodturner will find a good bandsaw a tremendous asset. The one shown here has a 380mm. (15in.) throat or distance from blade to vertical part of casing. It will deal efficiently with hardwoods or softwoods up to 178mm. (7in.) in thickness. Some designs call for tapered staves to be used, in which case, having decided what degree of taper to use only one side of each stave is tapered, thus saving considerable time (Fig. 5-5).

The tapered strips are glued and assembled, pressure being evenly applied by means of hose clamps, for example, which can be tightened by means of a bolt. Others utilize blanks made from untapered staves (Fig. 5-6). Some work will look best if all the staves are cut from the same sort of wood, but alternating dark and light staves can be employed, or thin strips of contrasting colored veneer can be introduced between the joints. A little ingenuity will be well rewarded.

It cannot be over-emphasized that the joints in work like this must be precise. Near enough is simply not good enough; even if luck is with the turner and the job stays in one piece until he has finished, there will be gaps in the joints, which will look most unsightly.

Once the work has been properly set up in the lathe, the turning is much as for any other spindle turning. When the blanks are prepared, they have open ends, and it is necessary to fit a base before the turning can begin. Fig. 5-7 shows the preparation of the base disc. When using the bandsaw, note that the guard and upper guide assembly must always

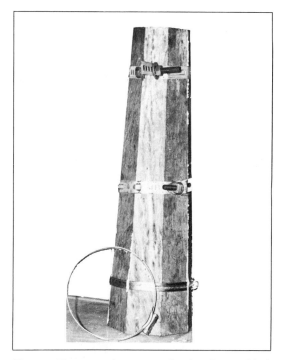

Fig. 5-5 The tapered strips are glued and assembled, pressure being applied by hose clamps or straps that can be tightened by means of a bolt.

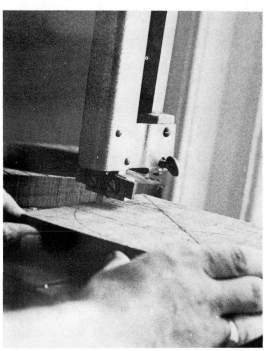

Fig. 5-6 Blanks can be made from strips which have not been tapered, as shown here; this will be more convenient for some types of container.

Fig. 5-7 Bandsaw being used to cut a disc for turning to make a tankard base.

Fig. 5-8 Completed disc cutting.

Fig. 5-9 Circular blanks cut from scrap timber to be turned into plugs.

Fig. 5-10 Blanks mounted on woodscrew chuck; tapered with deep-fluted bowl gouge.

be set close to the work surface to avoid injury to the hands (Fig. 5-8). Softwood or hardwood circular blanks are cut from scrap timber to be turned into plugs for mounting the blanks in the lathe, Fig. 5-9 and 5-10. The

blades I use are known as skip tooth, alternate teeth being missed out. I find best those blades with flexible backs and hardened teeth, with three points to 25mm. (1in.), and I braze my own with blade material cut from large rolls supplied in plastic dispensers. To do this, the blank is mounted in the machine with a tapered wooden plug in each end, holding it securely (Fig. 5-11). It may be helpful to make the plug smaller than the one shown, so that it will fit inside the blank. The tool rest is positioned across the right-hand end, and a rabbet is cut with the parting tool (Fig. 5-12). This must be done carefully, taking a small cut each time until the full rabbet width is achieved. The job can then be taken from the lathe.

Fig. 5-11 Mounted blank with plug in place at tailstock end.

Fig. 5-12 Cutting the rabbet.

A base can now be turned up on a woodscrew chuck with a matching rabbet, which is achieved by trial and error. The two parts are then glued firmly (Fig. 5-13), and after sufficient time has been allowed for them to set, the rough blank can be refitted to the woodscrew chuck, using three screws (Fig. 5-14) and a sharp scraper worked with light cuts to smooth the interior. Once this has been done and sanded, the usual tapered plug is fitted in the open end, tailstock supprt is given, and the outside is shaped (Fig. 5-15–17). With the blank securely mounted on a woodscrew chuck, the inside is shaped with a sharp

Fig. 5-15 The blank securely mounted, the outside is shaped with a sharp bowl gouge.

Fig. 5-16 The shaping continues.

Fig. 5-13 Base fitted and a piece of plywood placed over the open end of blank to allow pressure to be applied by cramp.

Fig. 5-17 The shape completed.

Fig. 5-14 With the base firmly glued in postion, the blank is mounted on a 64mm. (2½in.) woodscrew chuck.

scraper, then the plug is fitted, and the tailstock gives support while a 9mm. (⅜in.) deep-fluted gouge shapes the outside (Fig. 5-15). The shaping continues (Fig. 5-16). A sharp gouge used correctly will produce clean shavings and leave a smooth surface. The completed shape is shown in Fig. 5-17. All that now remains is to cut a handle and sand it to shape.

For those designs which incorporate a lid, the making and fitting is similar to that of the base, forming the rabbet on the lid disc first, then reversing the work on the chuck to do the shaping. When both lid and bottom section are turned, the lid can be fitted to the body, the tailstock brought up to support the job, and a final clean cut will mate the two parts. The knob is turned up separately and secured by means of a screw from the other side of the lid.

Cookie Jar

Among the type of articles attractive to produce by the builtup method are such items as cookie jars. First, inner and outer circles are scribed on a board (Fig. 5-18A), ready for the cutting of discs to be laminated into blanks for a cookie jar. Holes are drilled to permit the entry of a jigsaw blade. Fig. 5-18B shows the Stanley Vari-Speed saw removing disc centers while the plank is intact which makes for easy holding. Completion of the disc cutting can be done with the jigsaw, but a bandsaw is certainly quicker (Fig. 5-19).

The centers removed from the discs can be retained for use in other turning projects. Fig. 5-20–22 show a finished set of rings ready for assembly; plenty of glue is used, and an old paint brush makes a good applicator. Here rings of birch plywood have been placed between the thicker ones. Once assembled, pressure is applied by rapid action C clamps which I find extremely useful (Fig. 5-23). The finished blank has been mounted on a face-

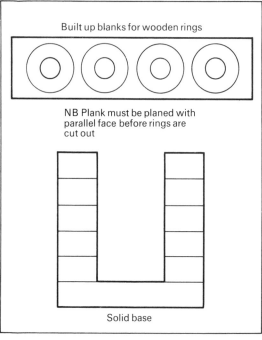

Built up blanks for wooden rings

NB Plank must be planed with parallel face before rings are cut out

Solid base

Fig. 5-18A—B Disc centers being removed (below).

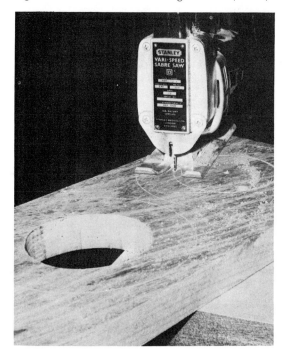

Fig. 5-21 Finished set of elm and afrormosia rings.

Fig. 5-19 Completed disc cutting.

Fig. 5-22 Rings of birch plywood have been placed between the thicker ones.

Fig. 5-20 Centers are removed.

Fig. 5-23 An assembly under pressure from C clamps.

43

Fig. 5-24 Finished blank mounted on face plate. Inside is partly turned.

Fig. 5-25 Tool rest inside job.

Finally, the lid should be constructed (Fig. 5-29–30). Fig. 5-31 shows the deep-fluted 9mm. (⅜in.) bowl gouge, brought to a fine edge, dealing effectively with the job. A scraper should not be used, as it would knock pieces out of the buildup. Fig. 5-32 shows the completed cookie jar still attached to the faceplate. Unless the wood is really well seasoned, a blank like this will move after it is taken into a warm house, and the plywood will protrude. If this occurs, the item can be remounted on the faceplate, trimmed up with a sharp gouge, and repolished.

Fig. 5-26 Turning of the outside is a job for the 9mm. (⅜in.) bowl gouge, working on its side with the bevel rubbing.

Fig. 5-27 Inside and outside completed, including sanding with fine paper and very fine steel wool.

plate (Fig. 5-24), and turning of the inside has been partly executed with a round-nosed scraper. The process should be continued until sides and base have been neatly blended. At this stage, beginners may benefit from positioning the tool rest inside the job so that less projection of the tool from the rest will be needed (Fig. 5-25).

Fig. 5-26–28 show turning of the outside, its completion, and the application of friction polish for finishing. The latter should be put on with cotton wool inside a soft cloth, using plenty of pressure to bring up a shine.

Fig. 5-28 Friction polish to finish.

Fig. 5-29 Roughly assembled blank for lid after trimming on bandsaw.

Fig. 5-30 Lid blank mounted on woodscrew chuck reading for turning.

Fig. 5-31 Deep-fluted 9mm. (⅜in.) bowl gouge, brought to a fine edge, will deal effectively with the job.

Fig. 5-32 Completed cookie jar still attached to the faceplate.

Egg cups seem to have a great fascination both for newcomers to woodturning and to the buying public. After a certain amount of practice they are not too difficult to make individually, but since they are normally in sets, this is often the first introduction to copy turning. The question of repeating a design can be left for the moment while a method of making the first design is considered.

Taking the simple design in Fig. 6-1A, the first job is to cut a square block of wood to the correct length (Fig. 6-2), mark the center at one end, make a hole with a bradawl, and fix the block firmly to a small woodscrew chuck, Fig. 6-3. The face diameter of this should not exceed 38mm. (1½in.). Care will be needed when screwing the block on to the chuck. It needs to be tight, but half a turn too much will strip the screw thread in the wood and defeat

WOODEN TABLEWARE 1

6

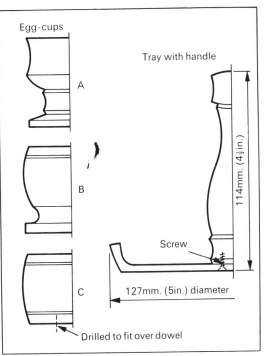

Fig. 6-1A—C

Fig. 6-2 Materials for a set of four egg cups. Disc and small square length will make tray and handle.

Fig. 6-3 Blocks for egg cups are best turned on a small woodscrew chuck that will not obstruct the cutting tools.

the object. The amount of tightening which can be done will vary with the density of the wood used, and one soon gets the feel of the thing. The screw used in the chuck should certainly not be smaller than a 1in. × No. 14 (25mm.).

Turn the block almost to a cylinder, clean up the end, making it slightly concave, trim the end grain with the chisel point, mark the center and push in a bradawl point, then sand and polish the surface, and reverse the block on the chuck. This gives a firm mounting and ensures that the cup will stand firmly on the breakfast tray. A few cuts with a sharp rough-

ing gouge will bring the block to a true cylinder, leaving it slightly over the required diameter. It can now be tapered towards the chuck.

Before any further work is done, the inside should be hollowed, a process which should always be carried out before the blank is weakened too much by shaping. The hollowing is done with a 6mm. (¼in.) spindle gouge ground to a short bevel and kept for this sort of purpose. The cut requires practice before it can be executed smoothly and efficiently, but once the knack has been acquired, it will be found very useful. It may be possible to complete the hollowing with the gouge, but it is likely that keeping the bevel rubbing will become difficult; if so, a really sharp, round-nosed scraper is brought in to finish the job with light cuts (this tool being at its best on end grain).

Some turners fit a plug to the cup at this stage and use the tailstock for support, but I have never found this to be necessary. All that remains with this particular shape is to cut the cove near the base with slicing cuts, using the 13mm. (½in.) gouge to do so.

Sets of egg cups call for careful work, but are not too hard to execute if no attempt is made to rush the job. It is worth considering here that it is far easier to make up sets of items like this if fairly large numbers are turned—say three or four dozen at a time—and the sets picked out from the ones closest matched.

Egg Trays

Wooden egg cups are often sold in small cardboard boxes, but these sets are not really complete without a tray or stand. One effective idea is to have a hole about 13mm. (½in.) in diameter through the bottom of each cup, and to make up a stand so that the cups can be slipped over the pin. This is rather like turning the base for a table lamp with a 13mm. (½in.) hole at the center into which a length of dowel is fitted with a spot of glue.

Circular trays are popular and easy enough to make. The disc is mounted on a large wood-screw chuck, trimmed to a circle of the required diameter with the deep-fluted 9mm. (⅜in.) gouge, and hollowed out with a sharp parting tool, making a series of cuts commencing at the outside until there is just a small amount of wood left at the center. This can be shaped to form a mount for the handle. It may be necessary to trim the bottom of the hollow with a square-ended scraper, to make quite sure that it is really flat, and the edge can be shaped with a gouge. After the handle is turned, it can be fitted with glue and a screw put through from underneath the tray.

The handle is turned up between centers using a piece of wood slightly longer than necessary, so that the waste can be parted off afterwards. Sharp tools and light cuts will now be essential, or the phenomenon known as ribbing will occur. This is in the form of spiral markings along the wood; a little support given to the work by the hand as the tool cuts will usually clear it up.

When all the essential work has been done to the handle, it is parted through as far as possible at each end, leaving about 6mm. (¼in.) to be sawed through by hand or on the bandsaw. The marks left by the saw are sanded off by hand.

Egg cups and other items which need cleaning after use must be given some suitable protective coating, so that they can be washed or wiped with a damp cloth. A few coats of polyurethane will do the trick. Since there is, of course, no set size for an egg, there will always be someone to tell you that the hole is not the right size. The only answer is to turn up a wooden egg on a woodscrew chuck and use this as a guide when hollowing.

Bowls

For some reason I have never been able to work up any genuine enthusiasm for bowl turning, perhaps because I am a parsimonious soul who hates to see so much wood wasted. Fortunately many people do like making them—indeed some make very little else.

As far as design is concerned, there is not a great deal to be said because the variety of shapes which can be thought up for bowls is rather limited. I have given a few examples, including two nut bowls and a little bowl with a lid (Fig. 6-4). Nut bowls are the most sought after, with the possible exception of salad bowls. I often think that people pick up a bowl and try to imagine what they would put into it if they bought it, then decide that it is too big or too small, and put it back— whereas what one does with a nut bowl is fairly obvious!

The one shown in Fig. 6-4C is very popular, and a little hammer to crack the nuts with enhances its attraction. I usually turn the hammer head on a woodscrew chuck, with the wood longer than needed, then part it off after shaping, leaving the waste in the chuck. The hole for the handle must be radial or it will look bad, and it can be drilled before the turning, if desired. If drilled afterwards, the

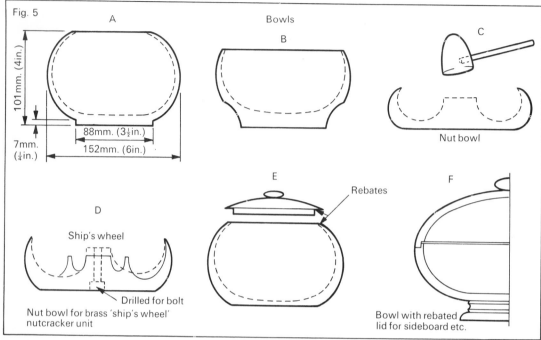

Fig. 5

A   Bowls   B   C

101mm. (4in.)

7mm. (¼in.)

88mm. (3½in.)
152mm. (6in.)

Nut bowl

D   E   Rebates   F

Ship's wheel

Drilled for bolt

Nut bowl for brass 'ship's wheel' nutcracker unit

Bowl with rebated lid for sideboard etc.

Fig. 6-4A—F

cylinder should be laid in a V-shaped groove cut in a scrap piece of softwood, the bottom of the V being centered to the point of a center drill.

Bowls with a brass ship's wheel nutcracker unit in the middle are attractive and useful and are normally turned as a sort of bowl within a bowl, so that the shells fall into the center recess instead of being mixed up with the nuts. Accessories like these are available through advertisements which appear in woodworking magazines.

Fig. 6-5 shows the initial stage in hollowing a mahogany nut bowl, using the gouge on its side. With a sharp bowl gouge, even a large bowl can be completely hollowed and shaped inside in a few minutes. Those who find a gouge difficult to control can manage with a

Fig. 6-5 Hollowing a mahogany nut bowl, using the gouge on its side.

scraper, keeping it flat on the tool rest and pivoting it to produce the radius. Never allow a scraper to point upwards inside a bowl (Fig. 6-6). If a good quality steel scraper is sharpened frequently—and correctly—a reasonable surface finish can be obtained on some

Fig. 6-6 Using a scraper, keeping it flat on the tool rest, and pivoting it to produce the radius.

Fig. 6-8 Applying sanding sealer to the nut bowl.

hardwoods. Note that the tool removes shavings—not dust (Fig. 6-7). Fig. 6-8 and 9 show the specific components required for the ship's wheel nut bowl and the application. of sealer. Fig. 6-10 shows the completed bowl.

Fig. 6-9 Components of Ship's Wheel nutcracker unit.

Fig. 6-7 A good quality steel scraper produces a reasonable surface finish on some hardwoods.

Fig. 6-10 A completed nut bowl fitted with a brass Ship's Wheel nutcracker unit.

There are ill-informed sources which state from time to time in books and articles that all faceplate work, particularly bowls, should be scraped. This is quite wrong, unless the statement is completed with "by those who cannot use gouges properly."

Scraping wood is never a good idea if it can be avoided, since it is dusty, tedious, and inefficient—quite apart from being incredibly slow. With sharp gouges, used properly, even a large bowl will be shaped both inside and out in well under an hour without great haste, leaving plenty of time for the final sealing and sanding process.

My bowl work is done with 9mm. (⅜in.) and 18mm. (¾in.) deep-fluted gouges, ground straight across at the end and kept very sharp. Fig. 6-11 shows how the gouge bevel must rub and the consequent steep angle of the tool. Most manufactured tool rests will not permit the gouge to be used correctly without considerable difficulty. A sharp bowl gouge can take quite heavy cuts without fear of digging in, if the bevel is correctly presented (Fig. 6-12).

Fig. 6-12 A sharp bowl gouge can take quite heavy cuts without fear of digging in, if the bevel is correctly positioned.

Fig. 6-11 How the gouge bevel must rub and the consequent steep angle of the tool.

I get the outside as smooth as possible with one of these, then trim out any marks left by the gouge with a scraper bar, which is a piece of flat, high-speed steel. This has no handle, and there is no really satisfactory method of fitting one, so it must have minimal projection from the tool rest. Never under any circumstances should this be used on the inside of a bowl. It will take shavings off so fine that they are almost like fluff, and the surface is left beautifully smooth.

Shaping the outside of a bowl should not take more than ten minutes if correct methods are employed. Heavy cuts tend to produce a rough surface, which can be corrected by sharpening the gouge and taking finer

Fig. 6-13 Correcting heavy cuts. If cut is too heavy, handle is lowered to correct fault.

Fig. 6-14 The bowl gouge used slightly on its side.

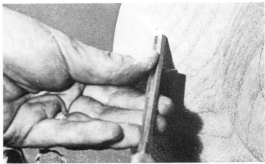

Fig. 6-15 Using a sharp 13mm. (½in.) spindle gouge on an awkward patch of grain.

cuts—which means lowering the handle a fraction (Fig. 6-13). The bowl gouge is used slightly on its side (Fig. 6-14). As in all turning, the cutting should be done from a large diameter to a smaller—never vice versa. The gouge travels in the direction of the flute. A really awkward patch of grain can sometimes be dealt with by using a sharp 13mm. (½in.) spindle gouge (Fig. 6-15). Care should be taken, however, because this tool can easily dig into the wood.

If the curve of the inside is such that the gouge can be used throughout with its bevel rubbing, so much the better, but in many cases this will not be possible, and a round-nosed scraper will be needed to finish the job. This is a pity, because there will be an immediate deterioration in the quality of the surface when the turner changes from the gouge to the scraper. He has, therefore, committed himself to spending time in putting this right after he has arrived at the shape.

Remember that the bottom of a bowl, like other articles which have been discussed, should be very slightly concave, for if there is a little high spot at the center, the finished job will be very unstable. The thickness of the bowl walls is to some extent a matter of taste.

Personally I feel that when the walls are turned very thin, the bowl loses that woody feel and has something of compressed cardboard about it when handled.

There is no special skill involved in getting these things extremely thin, nor any great merit, for the thinner they are the more fragile, and bowls do get dropped occasionally. Fig. 6-16–20 show the hollowing out of the bowl. Fig. 6-18 shows an alternative method of hollowing used on large bowls.

Fig. 6-18 Trough formed by alternate cuts from each side so bowl wall is finished before hollowing is completed.

Fig. 6-16 Close-up of the start of hollowing by trough method, gouge on its side.

Fig. 6-19 Opening up an ash bowl. Here the gouge works on the right-hand side of the job.

Fig. 6-17 Action shot of hollowing a bowl. The thickness of shavings produced by a good bowl gouge makes this a rapid process.

Fig. 6-20 Removal of center of African walnut bowl which has been hollowed by trough method. Final cuts are from edge to center.

Note that the outside of this bowl has been turned first, the wood then being reversed on the chuck for hollowing.

A really large lump of hardwood attached to a faceplate and revolving at a comparatively high speed must be quite an alarming sight to the beginner who has to approach it with his gouge, and I would strongly advise a novice to start off with tiny bowls, say about 152mm. (6in.) in diameter and 50mm. (2in.) in thickness. Softwood will do to practice with—if you can get a good finish on that you ought to be able to get it on anything. Sizes can be increased gradually as skill is acquired, and there will be fewer traumatic incidents.

Wood which has been damaged by gnawing actions from blunt tools is extremely difficult to bring to a good standard of finish with abrasive materials. This applies particularly in bowl work where the grain direction is changing all the way around. High-quality turned work depends on the tool work being good, and little abrasive action is called for.

Turning a single bowl is quite different from turning a matching set of six or so, if they are to be really accurate, and this sort of job is best left until the gouge feels like part of the arm. The time will come, however, when someone wants a large salad bowl and a set of small individual ones, and this will be a real test of skill.

Finally, a word on finishing. Bowls in continuous use require a good finish which is effective as protection and treatment for the wood, as well as giving a gloss if desired. Bowls which have been oil-finished should not be washed, but wiped out with a cloth and

Fig. 6-21 Lacquer sealer wiped over the inside of a bowl before sanding.

a little salad oil. Fig. 6-21 shows the liberal application of cellulose sealer to the inside of a bowl in preparation for sanding. Some woods will require several applications.

Fruit bowls (Fig. 6-22) are best finished with a brushing lacquer or with several coats of good quality polyurethane, each one being thoroughly sanded. The final coat is thinned down considerably for best results. If a high gloss is not required, the last coat can be rubbed lightly with very fine steel wool, grade 000.

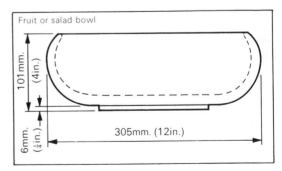

Fruit or salad bowl

101mm. (4in.)

6mm. (¼in.)

305mm. (12in.)

Fig. 6-22

Salad bowls can be treated as above, but are more often given an oil finish. Special oils can be purchased for the job. Oil finishes should be applied sparingly and worked well into the wood. Several light coats, each given a day or so to harden, will be far better than a thick application.

Fig. 6-23 Fruit bowl from a piece of builder's quality 178mm. × 75mm. (7in. × 3in.) pine.

FLOOR LAMPS

Floor lamps do need care if they are to look professional, and the production of the slow sweeping curves which occur over their length is by no means easy. There is also the fact that if a small table lamp goes wrong, it is a case of back to the drawing board, and not too much is lost. However, in the case of the larger lamp, the cost factor is considerably greater, and the task should be tackled slowly and carefully. If the tools are kept sharp and the cuts light, there need be no trouble, but remember that, whereas one can always cut off a little more, no way has yet been found to stick wood back when too much has been cut off!

Two possible designs for floor lamps are illustrated in Fig. 7-1 and 7-2. One point which ought to be dealt with at the start is that, since the two sections of the lamp stem are to be joined by a pin and a hole, the hole must be drilled before the turning starts (Fig. 7-3). It is done in the normal way, with the drill revolving slowly in the headstock, and the wood being fed to it by means of the tailstock, keeping a firm grip on the material. Make the hole reasonably deep, at least 25mm.–38mm. (1in.–1½in.), so that the joint will be really strong and there is no danger of the work falling apart (Fig. 7-4).

The pin on the end of the piece is turned with a sharp parting tool, taking a cut the width of the tool edge and repeating until the pin is long enough, using a pair of calipers to arrive at the desired diameter (Fig. 7-5). Be careful about the end of this cut nearest to the stem, which should be slightly undercut so that the two parts will meet with edge contact. If the parting tool is inadvertently sloped the wrong way, there will be an unsightly gap around the edge of the joint. Note also that the handle of the tool should be kept low, so that the bevel can rub and the edge can cut correctly. Holding the tool horizontal is a com-

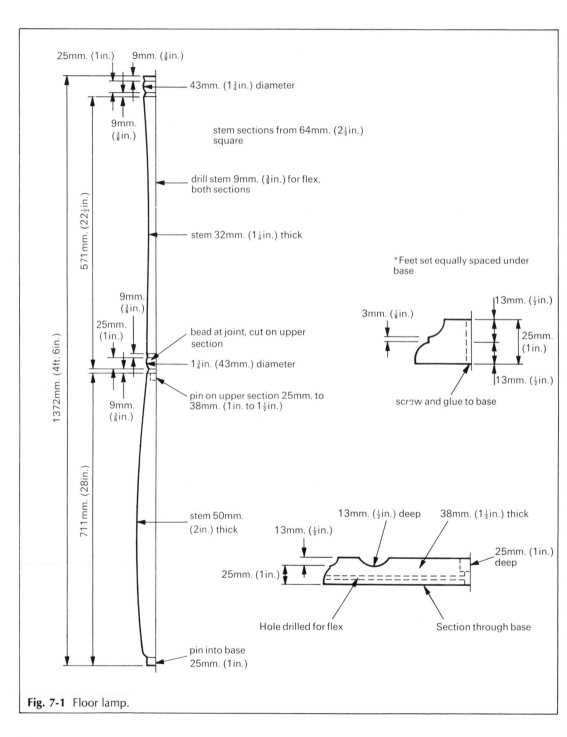

25mm. (1in.) 9mm. (⅜in.)

43mm. (1¾in.) diameter

9mm. (⅜in.)

stem sections from 64mm. (2½in.) square

drill stem 9mm. (⅜in.) for flex, both sections

stem 32mm. (1¼in.) thick

571mm. (22½in.)

*Feet set equally spaced under base

9mm. (⅜in.)

25mm. (1in.)

3mm. (⅛in.)

13mm. (½in.)

25mm. (1in.)

bead at joint, cut on upper section

1¾in. (43mm.) diameter

13mm. (½in.)

9mm. (⅜in.)

pin on upper section 25mm. to 38mm. (1in. to 1½in.)

screw and glue to base

1372mm. (4ft. 6in.)

711mm. (28in.)

stem 50mm. (2in.) thick

13mm. (½in.) deep   38mm. (1½in.) thick

13mm. (½in.)

25mm. (1in.) deep

25mm. (1in.)

Hole drilled for flex

Section through base

pin into base
25mm. (1in.)

Fig. 7-1 Floor lamp.

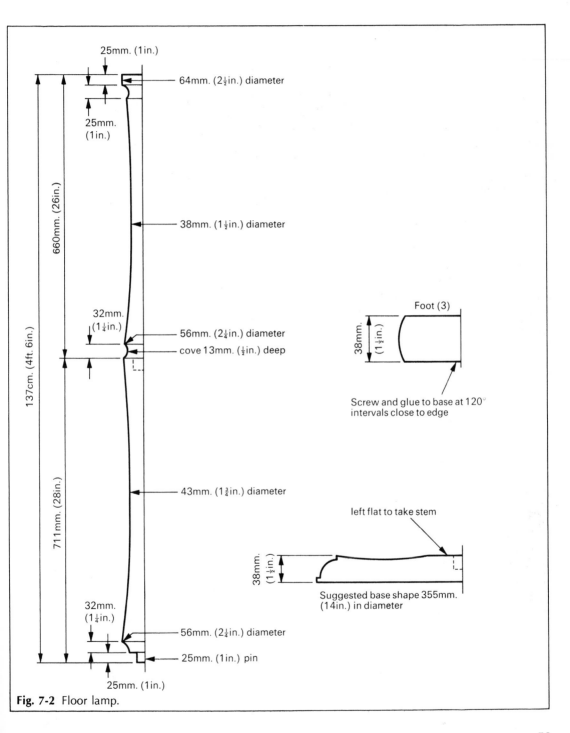

25mm. (1 in.)

64mm. (2½ in.) diameter

25mm. (1 in.)

660mm. (26 in.)

38mm. (1½ in.) diameter

137 cm. (4 ft. 6 in.)

32mm. (1¼ in.)

56mm. (2¼ in.) diameter

cove 13mm. (½ in.) deep

Foot (3)

38mm. (1½ in.)

Screw and glue to base at 120° intervals close to edge

711mm. (28 in.)

43mm. (1¾ in.) diameter

left flat to take stem

38mm. (1½ in.)

Suggested base shape 355mm. (14 in.) in diameter

32mm. (1¼ in.)

56mm. (2¼ in.) diameter

25mm. (1 in.) pin

25mm. (1 in.)

Fig. 7-2 Floor lamp.

Fig. 7-3 Wood bored at one end to take a pin, which will be turned on the mating section. The tailstock center fits into the hole nicely.

Fig. 7-5 Vernier caliper in use, checking diameter of partly turned pin that will fit into other section of stem. This is done with the work stationary, after the pins on the upper side of the tool have been set to fit the hole.

mon fault, which results in a scrape rather than a cut and blunts the edge very quickly.

The bottom section of the stem will also need to have the pin cut on it to locate in the base. This joint must be strong, or it will break the first time the lamp is knocked over. If the base is not sufficiently thick to give a strong tenon joint, a block of wood can be fitted underneath to give enough strength, this preferably being turned to a disc for neatness. Obviously, if this is done, it will be necessary to provide the lamp with three or four small feet around the edge of the base to lift the strengthener clear of the floor, but this is a simple job.

The normal height for a floor lamp is about 152.4cm. (60in.) to the bottom of the lamp holder, which is beyond the capacity of most modern lathes used in home workshops, even if the operator could cope with the ribbing and whipping problems. For this reason, the stem is made in two parts joined by means of a pin and a hole as described. The join should be made at a point where there is detail to

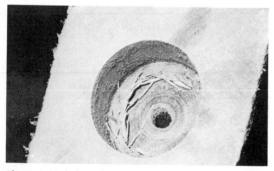

Fig. 7-4 Hole bored in square length of timber prior to mounting in lathe. Roughness at bottom can be removed with a chisel.

hide it, or in other words, the design should allow for the join.

The two square sections for the stem, each about 69cm. (27in.) long, will need to be drilled through for the wire prior to turning. Briefly, the job is done with the long-hole boring kit as supplied for many lathes, which is made up of an auger, a center-finding device, a counterbore, and a drilling jig. Setting up must be done with care, making quite sure that all clamps are tight before switching on the machine. The piece of wood being drilled is quite hefty, and a serious accident could result should it fly from the lathe. This does not mean that the operation is dangerous—I have performed it hundreds of times without trouble—but it must be done with care. Although on a fairly short length of timber it is possible to go right through from one end, this should not be tried on a long section even if the auger will reach, for the hole may be found to be inaccurate; if the auger is wandering, it may be quite a long way off by the time it reaches the other end.

The correct method is to drill a little over halfway, then reverse the wood on to the pin of the counterbore, which is used in place of the normal driving center, and complete the operation from the other end. This means that the hole at each end is central, and if there is any error, it will be where the two drillings have met. Once the procedure has been practiced, a few times, it will be found very simple and effective.

Both square sections are drilled, and the counterbore is left in the headstock to act as a driving center for the turning. This makes the centering of the material quite easy, as the pin is the same size as the hole.

Fig. 7-6 Material in position for turning one section of a floor lamp.

Fig. 7-6 shows material in position for turning one section of a floor lamp stem. Note that the timber has been pre-drilled for the wire and is being driven by a counterbore tool in place of the normal driving center. The counterbore has a pin which fits the drilled hole, so centering the wood.

A close-up of the driven end of the work. Fig. 7-7 shows how the nibs of the counterbore bite into the end grain. The knurled collar over the mandrel thread, immediately behind the counterbore, is to protect the thread from accidental damage and to facilitate removal of items fitted into the taper.

In common with any other spindle turning, the initial requirement is to run the wood to a cylinder using the roughing gouge. Here a very important point arises; in order to carry out the sort of turning being discussed, it is really necessary to have a tool rest which covers the full run of the lathe (Fig. 7-8). One section of the floor lamp stem has been rough turned to a cylinder. Note the 50mm. (2in.) gouge (vertical at right) which was used to do the job quickly. Tool rests are a problem for the beginner anyway, in that the manufacturers of lathes are engineers and persist in mak-

Fig. 7-7 Close-up of driven end of work, showing how the nibs of the counterbore bite into the end grain.

Fig. 7-8 One section of floor lamp stem rough-turned to a cylinder. Note the 50mm. (2in.) gouge (vertical at right) used for a fast job.

ing tool rests which are quite unsuitable for the craft—unless all the work is to be scraped. The ones which are illustrated here were made up for me years ago to my own design and have been copied by many people who

have seen them or tried them out while under my instruction. For turning long runs, a long tool rest is almost essential, for with a long slow curve, moving the rest during the cut will almost certainly cause a mark where the cut has been started and stopped.

The roughing down should be done in sections, not from one end of the square straight along to the other, though once the corners have been removed the cuts can be taken right through. The usual procedure can be adopted, taking the wood down to a straight cylinder which has a diameter about 2mm. ($1/16$in.) larger than the maximum required continuing the shaping from this. The roughing gouge is not suitable for working down into steep hollows because of its square end. If sharp, however, it can well be employed for most of the shaping of long items, like floor lamps, where the curves are mainly slow. Do make sure that the bevel really does rub all the time, and that handle is not, in fact, being held too high, or the work will suffer.

The best way to arrive at this happy state is to lower the handle until the cut stops, then raise it just sufficiently to start it again. Note also that if the tool is used square to the work, the edge is crossing the grain at right angles so producing an inferior cut. The gouge should point very slightly in the direction in which it is to travel, and be rolled slightly on to the same side. This gives a slicing cut, with the cutting edge at an angle to the grain, and the finish will be good. The turner should not be tempted to swing the cut through a hollow past the center. The tool must cut downhill; therefore, do not pass the center just becasue things are going well. They will get progressively worse if you do. Once the turning of a section of stem has been completed, it can be

Fig. 7-9 Stem section after completion of turning.

Fig. 7-11 Here the faceplate, carefully centered, is having its screw positions marked.

Fig. 7-10 Immediately after sealing and sanding, the job should be checked for any scratches which may be removed by hand-sanding with the grain—with the lathe switched off.

coated thoroughly with cellulose sealer while stationary, then sanded with fine paper when the sealer is dry (Fig. 7-9 and 7-10).

The base is a typical faceplate turning, where width and thickness are not critical and can be varied according to individual taste. Before the material for the base is mounted on the faceplate, it should be planed and checked for a flat surface. Screwing alloy faceplates to twisted wood results in twisted faceplates which are obviously undesirable. A relatively large blank such as this should be centered with maximum care when fitting to the plate (Fig. 7-11). This is to reduce the

initial vibration which is certain to be present until the disc has been trued up with a gouge. Some thought must also be given to the speed at which the turning is to be done. This must obviously be reduced from approximately 2000 r.p.m., employed on most spindle turning, or the peripheral speed of the wood will be excessive.

There is, incidentally, a danger here which may not immediately be apparent. Many years ago in my early woodturning days, I fitted up a piece of wood much like the one which would be used for this job and switched on the lathe without altering the speed. This proved to be a tactical error, for there was a hidden split in the blank and the centrifugal force was too much for it. The wood broke and I was lucky not to be standing in line with the piece which flew off, so the lesson is obvious. The speed must be reduced to reasonable r.p.m.; if it is not, the wood will be traveling far too fast to be cut properly, even if it does not break. A high speed on the edge of a disc like this will create great frictional heat, burning and softening the edge of the tool. A speed of about 750–1000 r.p.m. should be workable.

63

With the tool rest firmly fixed, the edge is trimmed to a true disc of the desired shape using a 9mm. (⅜in.) deep-fluted gouge, with the handle held low enough to permit the bevel to rub correctly. The tool rest is now moved round to the face of the job, which is cleaned up and leveled with a few cuts from the center to the edge (Fig. 7-12), and the pin which was cut on the lower part of the stem is measured with a Vernier caliper. This measurement is transferred to the wood by applying the points of the caliper carefully as it revolves. Fig. 7-13 shows the continued base turning. Fairly rough, heavy cuts have been used to arrive at the shape, and the rings so formed on the work will be removed by light slicing cuts with a freshly sharpened gouge.

Fig. 7-13 Turning of base continues. Fairly rough, heavy cuts have been used to arrive at the shape, and the rings so formed on the work will be removed by light, slicing cuts with a freshly sharpened gouge.

The area so marked is hollowed out carefully with a parting tool, leaving a thin layer of wood at the bottom, so that the tool cannot break through and strike the faceplate. This layer can be cut out after the turning with a craft knife or a sharp chisel. Another approach would be to have a piece of softwood between work and faceplate so that the tool could be taken right through, but this sometimes results in spelching or breaking of the wood where the tool emerges.

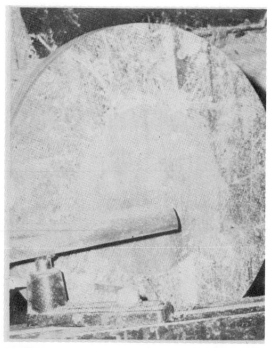

Fig. 7-12 A cut from the center to the edge, here shown half completed, will clean up the wood so that it can be examined for cracks, nails, or other hazards.

When the hole has been cut, calipers are used again to measure accurately the diameter of the lamp stem at the point where it will meet the base, and to transfer this measurement to the wood. It will now be possible to ensure

Fig. 7-14 Lathe table set up for drilling a lamp base for the wire.

that the area beneath the stem sits tightly down on the base. This slight concavity can be produced with one stroke of the gouge. The shaping is quite straightforward, the deep-fluted faceplate gouge is used, and the job can be done entirely with this tool. If it is deemed necessary to scrape, the results will not be too bad on a workpiece of this nature.

Sanding, sealing, and polishing follow in the normal way, care being taken to avoid the use of a grade of abrasive paper which is too coarse and so scratches the work. If these appear and are deep, they will be extremely difficult to remove, and a great deal of unnecessary time will be wasted in trying.

A final job is the drilling of a hole through the base to accommodate the wire, though in the absence of a suitable drill the wire can be run in a groove cut across underneath. This can best be done by using a support table giving a truly horizontal surface on which the work

can be fed to the drill (Fig. 7-14). Many lathes have such tables as optional extras. The assembly of the lamp should be done carefully, for it is always a great pity to spoil a good job by haphazard assembly. Run the wire through both base and stem sections before gluing up and secure it so that it cannot slip back again. The glue used should be a very strong one, since there is little likelihood of the lamp needing to be taken apart again, and I normally use something like Epoxy for these jobs.

In fitting the socket, as with other lamps, a ⅛″ pipe tap is used to cut a thread to accept that on the brass nipple (Fig. 7-15), which can then be screwed in with the fingers and the socket attached to it. This is, of course, preferable to the practice of many workers who knock in lamp nipples with a hammer, or glue them into holes which are drilled too large.

Fig. 7-15 It is best to thread the lamp nipple into an 8mm. (⁵/₁₆in.) hole which has a thread cut by a 9mm. (⅜in.) Whitworth tap.

There are numerous articles which the turner can make under this heading, some of which have already been described in chapter six. The finish on the work should be really first class, for shoddy items with scratches and rough patches are not welcome anywhere. For this reason, although I would agree that scrapers make a far better job on faceplate work than between centers, they should still be used as little as possible. The marblelike smoothness of a true cut from a sharp edge is the quickest and surest way to success.

Some of this tableware is very easy to make once the basics have been mastered. Things like butter or jam dish holders, cheese boards, teapot stands and so on, are really just discs of wood with a limited amount of elementary shaping done to them, with a finish applied. Salt shakers, pepper mills, or sugar bowls, on the other hand, are more difficult but most satisfying if carefully made.

In most forms of turning, it pays to spend a few hours now and then making up blanks for future use. Discs of seasoned wood, cut as accurately as possible on the bandsaw, can be stored more or less indefinitely if there is no woodworm about. Beware of prepared discs made from partly seasoned wood which are very likely to develop nasty splits while drying out. If discs are marked out by drawing round a circular template, this should have a hole at the exact center so that a bradawl can be pushed through into the work, providing an accurate center location for the eventual mounting of the wood. An alternative is to use a large pair of dividers, the leg of which will automatically mark the center.

WOODEN TABLEWARE 2

Simple Butter or Jam Dish Holders

Glass containers for jam, pickles, butter, etc. can be obtained from woodworking accessory suppliers and certain specialist sources which advertise in the woodworking press. These are not expensive, but if you are going into production of this sort of thing for a living you will, of course, need to find a wholesale supplier from whom you can buy in bulk. Fig. 8-1 shows various designs for holders.

A suitable disc is prepared and mounted on a screw chuck. It will not be necessary or desirable to have the screws going deeply into the wood. If three screws are used in the chuck they need not penetrate the work more than 9mm. (⅜in.) and the holes they make can be hidden by the application of green baize.

As with any disc, the outside is trimmed first with a sharp gouge to a true circle of the required diameter and any shape called for on the outside of the job is cut. The tool rest is now swung round to the front of the wood, which is leveled and cleaned up with light cuts from the same tool. Before going any further, it will be necessary to mark exactly the outer edge of the area to be hollowed with a pencil or the point of a chisel. The hollowing is now done with a parting tool, one tool's width at a time being taken almost to full depth, until the whole area is roughly hollowed.

With the lathe stationary, the glass container is tried for fit. It should be a trifle slack to allow for possible shrinkage of the wood after turning. If the hole is right the bottom of it can be cleaned up and made truly flat by means of a square-ended scraper with a very sharp edge. It is as well on this sort of work to check that the sides of the hollowed area are square to the surface of the disc, not sloping to form a taper. Final shaping can now be carried out and the machine stopped before sanding the

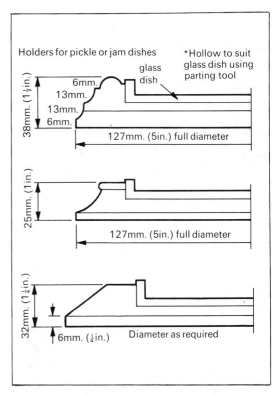

Fig. 8-1

wood to permit a detailed examination of the surface of the job. Any defects found should be corrected with sharp tools—not optimism and sandpaper!

Small wooden dish containers like Fig. 8-1 should take between five and ten minutes to make, once the knack has been acquired.

Cheese Board
with Inlaid Tile

After making the article we have just discussed, the cheese board with inlaid tile will present no real problems, since it is basically

Fig. 8-2 Elm disc partly turned for cheese board with tile inset. Take care that no rough patches are left around the edge.

Fig. 8-5 A few patches of contact cement will hold the tile firmly in place.

Fig. 8-3 Board has been recessed to take tile insert, starting with parting tool, removing central area with bowl gouge, and trimming recess flat with square-ended scraper.

Fig. 8-6 The finished cheese board—an attractive item for any table.

Fig. 8-4 Tile is tried for fit, which should be a little slack to allow for shrinkage.

a larger version of the same thing (Fig. 8-2–6). The recess for the tile will be formed in the same manner as the one for the glass container and the deep-fluted 9mm. (⅜in.) gouge will do the shaping, including the cutting of the trough for the crackers. If the inexperienced turner finds himself getting into difficulties with this part of the operation he can revert to a sharp, round-nosed scraper, but here he should bear in mind that this is only a temporary method to be used until practice has given the skill required to do the job properly. Another cheese board design is shown in Fig. 8-7.

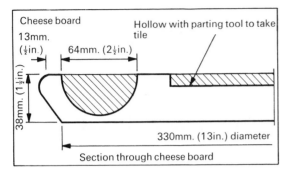

Fig. 8-7

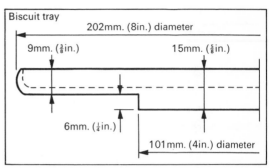

Fig. 8-8

For the cheese cutter stainless steel wire is used attached to a brass screw set in a brass cup fitting. The little toggle can be turned up between centers, the waste portion at each end being cut off afterwards. Tiles for this sort of job can be obtained in various sizes with a wide range of designs. They are not cheap, but a cheap tile would spoil a good piece of work.

Cracker Tray

This is a more advanced piece of wood-turning and an example of the fact that it is not always the most complicated shape which is the most difficult to produce (Fig. 8-8). The immediate problems are that wood-screws cannot be used to hold the workpiece because it is much too thin and that its lack of thickness will create a need for extremely sharp edges and very careful cuts. If the tray is made too thick it will feel and look awkward, and it may be necessary to make a fair number of these before the process becomes easy.

If screws cannot be used in the workpiece the best alternative is to attach the job to the lathe on a woodscrew chuck in the normal way, to shape the underside of the tray first, making a good job of it, and then polish. it. The base is made with a clear-cut edge, and the bottom of the base is made slightly concave.

The job can now be taken from the chuck, and a spare piece of hardwood mounted in its place. This is recessed carefully with a parting tool to accept the base of the turned tray as a tight drive fit, making sure that the workpiece beds down all round the edge of the base and is not twisted in the wooden chuck. If the homemade chuck is not quite tight enough, it can be wetted inside to swell the grain and give a good grip. Alternatively, a piece of paper can be used as packing.

This form of mounting seems to worry some beginners, who expect the job to go into orbit at any moment. In fact the frictional grip provided all round the edge of the base is quite sufficient for the purpose, and it is rare for anything like this to come out of the chuck if fitted properly in the first place.

Many bowls are turned in this fashion to avoid the screw holes which normally show on the base and to avoid the danger of cutting too deeply and striking the screws during the

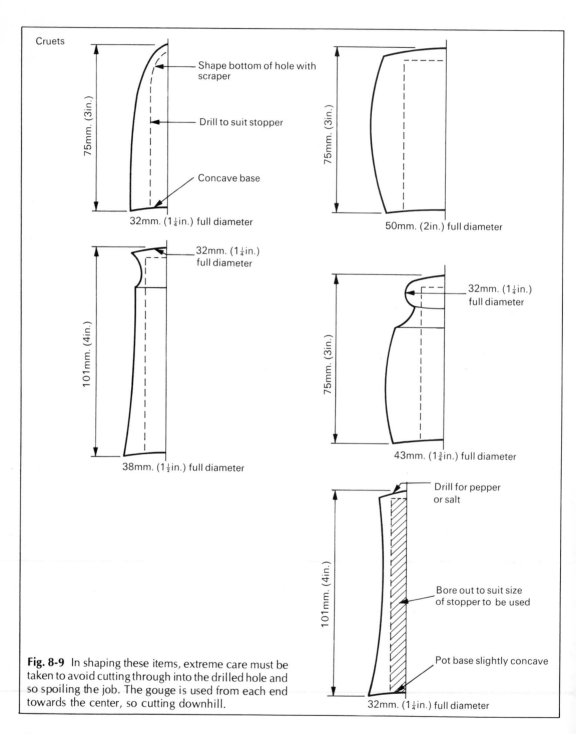

Cruets

Shape bottom of hole with scraper

Drill to suit stopper

Concave base

75mm. (3in.)

32mm. (1¼in.) full diameter

50mm. (2in.) full diameter

75mm. (3in.)

32mm. (1¼in.) full diameter

101mm. (4in.)

38mm. (1½in.) full diameter

32mm. (1¼in.) full diameter

75mm. (3in.)

43mm. (1¾in.) full diameter

Drill for pepper or salt

Bore out to suit size of stopper to be used

Pot base slightly concave

101mm. (4in.)

32mm. (1¼in.) full diameter

Fig. 8-9 In shaping these items, extreme care must be taken to avoid cutting through into the drilled hole and so spoiling the job. The gouge is used from each end towards the center, so cutting downhill.

turning. Unless the gouge can be handled with reasonable skill, it may be best to do the hollowing of the tray with a round-nosed scraper, keeping this either horizontal or pointing slightly downwards, and sharpening it frequently. When the wood is becoming thin, the sound of the cutting will alter, the note rising, and if heavy cuts or blunt edges are used the wood will bend away from the tool and the flexing will create an irregular surface. This can only be overcome by working slowly and lightly. Any attempt to hurry the proceedings will ruin the work.

Salt and Pepper Shakers

These are made by drilling a hole in a small block of wood, using a drill of a size to suit the stopper which is to be fitted. Rubber stoppers or corks can be employed for the purpose. The intended shape of the outside must be borne in mind when drilling, of course, or the curving of the end may cut into the drilled hole. The hole for the salt, or holes in the case of a pepper shaker can be drilled into the end of the square before turning if desired, making sure that they go through into the hollow interior. The usual turning method is to mount the block, which is about 13mm. (½in.) over length, between centers, with the tailstock center running in the drilled hole. The job is then brought to a cylinder, shaped, and the end cut to shape with the point of a skew chisel.

After sanding and polishing, the waste is cut off with a fine-toothed handsaw, and the cut surface is sanded smooth by hand. Fig. 8-9 gives various cruet designs.

Mustard Pots

Mustard containers made from blue glass are available from turnery suppliers and a little mustard pot is not difficult to make, although the lid is a more intricate job (Fig. 8-10). The wooden pot is turned up from a square block on a woodscrew chuck, the wood having been predrilled to depth for the container, and the drilled hole being widened as required with a parting tool. The square is turned to a cylinder and shaped with a spindle gouge and chisel point, and a rabbet is cut to accept the lid. The latter job calls for very careful and light cutting with a parting tool. The system here also is to have the square block over length, so that when the pot is completed it can be cut off with the parting

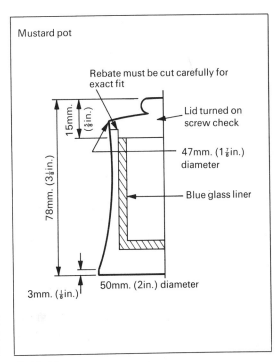

Fig. 8-10

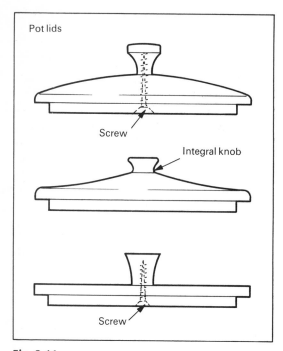

Fig. 8-11

tool, leaving a waste portion attached to the chuck.

For the lid (Fig. 8-11), a small block is fitted to the screw chuck and turned to a cylinder of appropriate size. The lid is then shaped on the end of the block with gouge and chisel, and a rabbet is cut to match that on the top of the pot. Very careful measuring and cutting will be required for this. After sanding and polishing, the lid is parted off and the bottom surface is hand sanded and polished. The small aperture to take the handle of the mustard spoon can best be made with a round file.

The tray to hold the cruet is very small, and it can be made by turning it up as part of a disc on a screw chuck and parting it off after polishing. The bottom will normally be covered with green baize; if not, a little hand

sanding will smooth it off sufficiently for polishing or varnishing.

Jam or Marmalade Jar Containers

Making a jam or marmalade jar container from a solid block entails a fair amount of work, but these are attractive items and very popular (Fig. 8-12). This is one of those jobs for which I prefer to use a blank built up from strips, as described earlier, but both methods should be practiced. If a solid block is used, it is drilled out at slow speed with a large diameter saw-tooth pattern bit to the necessary depth, this hole being enlarged to final size by turning. The interior is deep in relation to the width, however, and the parting

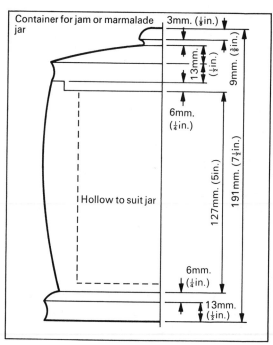

Fig. 8-12

tool cannot cope adequately with the task. An ordinary straight-ended scraper could be used.

A few years ago I designed a tool for just such operations which serves well. It was made from a very stout old file, in spite of my general views on grinding these things up to make scrapers, but I would certainly have preferred the same tool made in tool steel. What is needed is a suitable piece of steel about 355mm. (14in.) long and 18mm. (¾in.) square. This is ground; reasonable ability with the grindstone will be necessary for good results. The idea is that the tool cuts with its leading edge, but the side is also sharpened and trims the cut. This works well, and I only wish I could find someone to make me a few from good steel, with tangs so that they could be fitted into handles.

Do not attempt to use all the edge at once with these homemade tools because the cut will be too heavy; in fact, up to 3mm. (⅛in.) of the cutting edge is used. The thickness of the metal is such that the unusual amount of projection off the tool rest will not cause whipping or flexing, which could be dangerous.

In this sort of work one develops a feel for what is going on. This is essential because it is quite impossible to see. The rubbish which is cut away cannot escape and the interior becomes reminiscent of a bird's nest. One thing to be watched is that the bottom is kept smooth and that it blends well into the walls or sides. For such a container, the top will be rabbeted and a lid made along the same lines as those employed on the mustard pot.

Sugar Bowl and Spoon

The sugar bowl shown in Fig. 8-13 is similar to the one featured in *Modern Woodturning*, but I have included it because it has always been much admired, and it is the little spoon which gives it its charm. The shape of the bowl is pleasing; it is turned with a 9mm. (⅜in.) deep-fluted bowl gouge on a woodscrew chuck, using the methods described under bowl turning earlier in the book.

The spoon is easy to make, and the bowl is turned on the end of a short length of wood on a scew chuck, as much of the curvature being put on as possible. The shape is finally trimmed by hand-sanding after the workpiece has been parted off. The handle is turned between centers and fitted into a hole drilled in the bowl using a strong adhesive. Another design is shown in the lower half of Fig. 8-13.

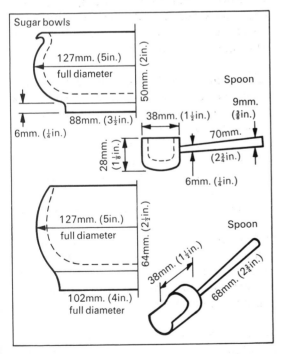

Fig. 8-13

There is no doubt that a set of goblets made from an attractive timber, such as yew, is a most striking thing and a really good set is the ambition of many amateur turners. Designs are shown in Fig. 9-1 and 9-2. Unfortunately, this sort of woodturning calls for a fair amount of skill, coupled with patience, for it cannot be hurried without spoiling the job.

If yew is chosen, and I have used it to good effect in the past, it must be prime, well-seasoned stuff, free of cracks. Yew is an excellent timber for the turner, it cuts well and polishes beautifully, quite apart from possessing striking beauty in its grain. Unfortunately, however, it is hard to obtain, expensive, and likely to have a multitude of tiny cracks within it, some of which may not be detectable until the turning is well under way, or even almost complete. This can be disappointing, but the chance is, in my view, worth taking. Other woods can be used, of course, both home grown and imported, and dark walnut can look good, though this again is not cheap. I have used wych elm which, if it can be found, has attractive grain. It is fun to experiment with timbers.

This is another job for the larger of the wood-screw chucks with three screws. Use a block longer than the intended height of the goblet so that the job can be parted off from the waste when it is finished. If this is not done, the base part will have to be left fairly thick to accommodate the screws and so may look clumsy.

Turning of this nature is delicate—there is no room for ham-fisted work, and the nearer the end of the job one gets, the greater is the danger that a sudden inept move may cause trouble. This should not put anyone off. The answer is to work steadily, always using very sharp tools and light cuts.

Some of my students seem to have difficulty in judging what constitutes a light cut. A cut

CUPS AND GOBLETS

Cups and goblets

Fig. 9-1

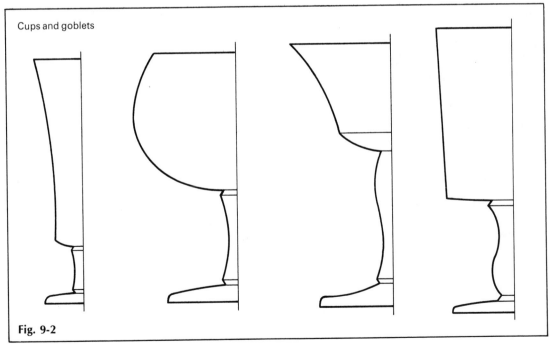

Cups and goblets

Fig. 9-2

is a cut, made with the bevel rubbing and the edge removing a shaving, no matter how thin. Rubbing the tool about on the surface, removing dust occasionally, is not the same thing at all. It will create tremendous frictional heat which will soften the cutting edge even if the dreaded blue mark does not appear on the metal. All cuts in woodturning have to be deliberate.

The approach is straightforward. The block for the goblet is firmly mounted on the chuck, and it is as well to ensure that its ends are square before mounting it. It is run down to cylindrical form with the roughing gouge; the hollowing of the interior is done first, before any shaping has weakened the material.

Use a 6mm. (¼in.) spindle gouge for this which must be sharp and, if the interior shape makes it necessary, the job can be finished off with a very sharp round-nosed scraper, cutting lightly. Only when the interior is satisfactory is it sanded thoroughly. The inside surface has to be right at this stage because it will be difficult, if not impossible, to work on it after the outside is turned.

Having completed the inside, a wooden plug with a slight taper is fitted into it, or a rounded piece of wood which fits the inside shape to some degree, and the tailstock is brought up to support the work for the remainder of the time. The tapered plug will do the job, but great care must be taken to see that the pressure of the tailstock on it does not

cause the edge of the goblet to split as the thickness of the wood decreases, which can easily happen. The sides of a goblet, especially around the rim, are very thin and care must be taken accordingly.

Turning the outside is fairly easy if done with proper methods, but in his anxiety to arrive at a nice thin job, the turner must be wary of cutting through the work, which can happen quite easily.

The curvature of the outside is best finished with a sharp skew chisel, using the smoothing cut, but this is difficult for anyone but an experienced turner, because rolling such a curve is far from easy. A 13mm. (½in.) spindle gouge could be used and will make a good job if it is sharp and the bevel kept firmly in contact with the wood.

The area between the base and the bottom of the cup part is roughed out by making two parting tool cuts and taking the waste wood between them out with the edge of a chisel. This leaves room for the shaping of the base, stem, and bottom of the cup. The detail at top and bottom of the stem is put in afterwards. Naturally, the hardest part of making a set of anything is in making them all alike, but goblets are not the best things to practice this on; it would be better to make a start with egg-cups or simple chess pawns.

The method outlined above can also be used for dice shakers, spill holders, and cup-like objects.

DESIGNS
FOR THE
KITCHEN

10

For those who are attracted by a slow but rewarding project involving a simple approach to copy turning, a set of spice containers to fit into an easily made rack may have considerable appeal.

The turning of the containers is a protracted business, but this sort of project need not be undertaken with a view to early completion, and the number of containers used is a matter for the individual.

The idea is by no means new. Basically it is a matter of turning little wooden boxes with lids, the lower parts of the boxes having a groove turned in them (Fig. 10-1A). They are bored out on a lathe with a multi-spur. Final sizing and cleaning up is done with a sharp scraper. The rack consists of a board with pieces of dowel projecting from it, spaced so that the boxes can be slid between, the dowels fitting into the grooves (Fig. 10-1B). The board is prepared from 13mm. (½in.) material, the length of which will vary according to the number of jars. Drill 6mm. (¼in.) into the board and glue the dowels in position (Fig. 10-1C). The width of the board is approximately 101mm.–114mm. (4in.–4½in.). The forward ends of the dowels are shaped on a disc sander. This will require accurate work or the job will look sloppy, but if the process is not hurried, there should be no trouble.

The bottom sections of the boxes are turned from small blocks of wood on a screw chuck, leaving sufficient length to permit the job to be parted off afterwards. The block is drilled out almost to depth in the manner described earlier, with a drill mounted in a chuck in the tailstock. The hole is then enlarged to the required size and a rabbet is cut to allow for the fitting of the lid. A small, tapered plug is fitted in the opening so that the tailstock can

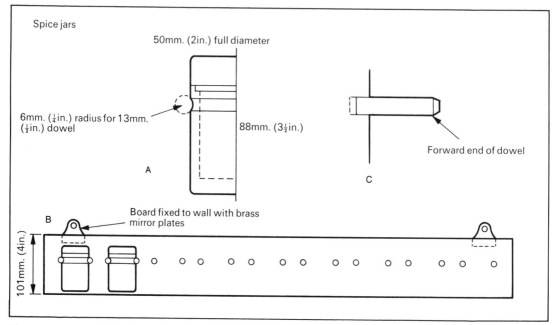

Fig. 10-1

be used for support, and the block is run down to the necessary shape and size. The groove is a cove which is cut with a 13mm. (½in.) spindle gouge after it has been carefully marked out.

Before the boxes are parted off, the slight curvature at the bottom is put on with the point of a skew chisel using a slicing cut. The lids are really just shorter boxes and are made in the same way, taking care over the cutting of the matching rabbets.

Barometer and Thermometer

Various forms of barometer and thermometer units can be obtained through the turnery suppliers. One design which I have found to

be very popular is the vaguely doorknob shaped variety which, when turned, has a slightly nautical aspect (Fig. 10-2). It is turned on a screw chuck, and by now it must be apparent just how useful these chucks are.

The block is turned to a cylinder, and the shaping is done with a spindle gouge and chisel. No scraping will be needed, the curve being rolled round with either the skew or the gouge. After a good sanding and polishing, the job is taken from the machine and the section is cut off at an angle on the bandsaw or by hand. When the surface of this has been sanded smooth, the thermometer unit is fixed in position with adhesive, and the job is done but for the application of some green baize to the base. Another design is shown in Fig. 10-3. These thermometer units are made two at a time by split turning. Two rectangular pieces are glued together with brown paper

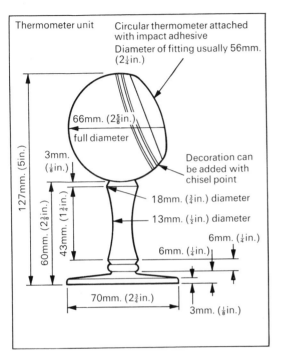

Fig. 10-2

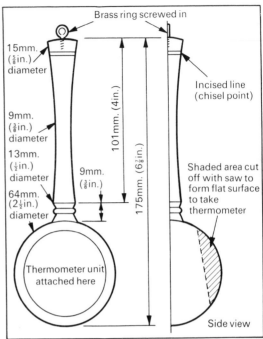

Fig. 10-3

in the joint so that they can be split apart after turning. The dried glue is removed on a belt or disc sander.

The making of a barometer unit along the lines of that illustrated in Fig. 10-4 is a job which can be done quite quickly with a most effective result. It is interesting because it is much like the making of circular cases for clocks.

A block of wood of suitable thickness is screwed to the faceplate, turned to a true circle of the correct size, and the face cleaned up with a couple of light cuts from a sharp faceplate gouge. The area to be hollowed is carefully marked out and the parting tool is used to get the job under way, working from the marked line towards the center, one cut at a time. It is not advisable to attempt to go the

full depth in one pass because the tool will become overheated. When the excavation is almost to the right depth, it can be cleaned up with a square-ended scraper to level the bottom.

It is best to have the mechanism a good fit, but not a tight one. It is a good idea to use some paper packing to take up any slack, for the wood may shrink slightly, rendering it impossible to remove the mechanism, which may be necessary from time to time for adjustment. This adjustment is quite simple, a screw being provided at the back of the barometer itself.

When the hollowing has been done, the block can be shaped. It will be best to use a deep-fluted faceplate gouge for this, as it is perhaps less likely to dig in than a spindle tool be-

79

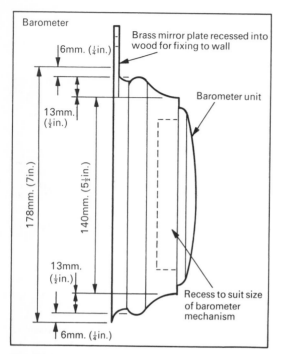

Barometer

Brass mirror plate recessed into wood for fixing to wall

6mm. (¼in.)

Barometer unit

13mm. (½in.)

178mm. (7in.)

140mm. (5½in.)

13mm. (½in.)

Recess to suit size of barometer mechanism

6mm. (¼in.)

Fig. 10-4

cause of its shape. It is used on its side, always traveling in the direction of the flute, taking slicing cuts, and leaving a fine surface.

Barometers of this type need a small brass plate fitted to the top rear, so that they can be hung on a wall.

Egg Stands

The egg stands illustrated are a popular gift item and they look much more attractive than the plastic type which is now so common. Fashion trends today favor stands in pine, but remember that the proper turning of this material to a really smooth finish is no job for a complete beginner.

The provision of templates made from plywood make the project quite simple. They are merely discs of appropriate sizes with small holes drilled through so that the hole center positions can be marked on the wood. They can have either one or two tiers. The drilling can be done on a lathe using the tailstock to feed the wood to a multi-spur bit, but some scrap wood will be needed as backing material to prevent the workpiece from spelching, or breaking away, as the cutter emerges. Alternatively, of course, a center drill can be used.

The stem parts of these egg stands are rather nice fiddly little spindle turnings, all gouge and chisel work. Two or three coats of polyurethane after assembling the parts with a good glue, and the result will grace any kitchen. Procedure is illustrated in Figs. 10-5 through 10-10.

In Fig. 10-5 a disc of parana pine is shown after it has been turned and rubbed with steel wool. The disc must now be drilled for the egg holes. The egg rack section is fed to a sharp multi-spur bit, Fig. 10-6, which revolves at 500–700 r.p.m. The tailstock is used

Fig. 10-5 Disc of parana pine after turning and rubbing with steel wool.

Fig. 10-6 Feeding the egg-rack section to a sharp multi-spur bit.

Fig. 10-7 Hole to accept the pin on the central stem is bored.

Fig. 10-8 Small piece of wood turned to cylinder between centers and marked out ready for turning of center spindle sections.

Fig. 10-9 Turning of the spindle sections is done with a 13mm. (½in.) spindle gouge.

Fig. 10-10 Trial dry assembly of parts.

to force the job forward—note the scrapwood backing. In Fig. 10-7 the center hole to accept the pin on the central stem is bored in the same manner, using a spade bit revolving at about 2000 r.p.m. Next a small piece of wood is turned to a cylinder between centers and marked out in preparation for the turning of the center spindle section (Fig. 10-10). This is turned with a 13mm. (½in.) spindle gouge (Fig. 10-9), always cutting between the center of the cutting edge and the corner. Finally, the parts are assembled dry (Fig. 10- 10). The pins should be a snug fit in the holes and the inside of the egg holes may need final sanding by hand.

Figs. 10-11 through 10-13 show completed items. Fig. 10-11 illustrates clearly the striking grain of yew as well as one of its major snags—the frequency of cracks.

Fig. 10-12 Six-egg rack turned in yew.

Fig. 10-11 Striking grain of yew.

Fig. 10-13 Rack for twelve eggs has seven holes at bottom, five at top.

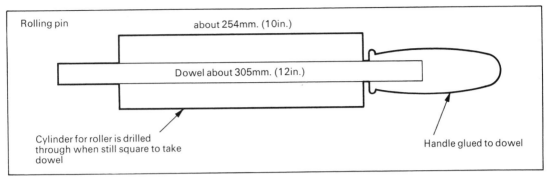

Rolling pin   about 254mm. (10in.)

Dowel about 305mm. (12in.)

Cylinder for roller is drilled
through when still square to take
dowel

Handle glued to dowel

Fig. 10-14

Rolling Pin

The rolling pin (Fig. 10-14) is a good example of straightforward spindle turning which calls for care in getting the handles exactly alike and for some drilling through the main part. This is normally done by drilling from each end in the lathe so that the two holes meet, but those with no facilities for this may like to try another approach which can be used for other similar operations.

The square length which is to become the body of the rolling pin is made up from two rectangular pieces glued firmly together, these having been grooved on one face, so that when they are put together there is a hole right through the blank. If preferred, this can be stopped a little short of the ends so that centering in the lathe is facilitated; the ends can be drilled afterwards. If the hole goes right through before turning, it will be necessary to plug both ends with scrap wood, which is removed after turning.

The making of the body is a simple matter of turning down to a straight cylinder and cleaning up the end grain with a chisel point. The rod can be an ordinary piece of dowel, or you can try your hand at turning it up.

The handles are turned from blocks between centers and parted off after sanding, but these blocks should be pre-drilled at one end to give a suitable hole to take the dowel. Finish can be polyurethane or wax.

Designs for these articles do not pose any real problems (see Fig. 11-1). What is required is a flat board recessed at the center, and undercut around the edge to facilitate lifting. The shapes of ordinary plates are as good a guide as anything, but it may be as well to have a few thoughts on how the job is set up and carried out. It will be appreciated that work of this kind is often quite thin, and the use of screws into the wood has to be discarded. Two methods are commonly used, and the best idea is to try out both.

For the first system the discs should be cut from a board which has been planed so that the surface is smooth and the faces are parallel. A smaller circle of softwood is glued to the disc, taking care to fix it centrally and sandwiching a piece of brown (kraft) paper in the glued joint, so that after turning is finished, the softwood can be split away easily by means of a chisel and mallet. The back of the job is then cleaned up by sanding and polished by hand. With this method the job is set up on a faceplate with four screws into the softwood.

As an alternative the hollow wooden chuck method can be employed, the discs being fitted into a recess cut in the face of a piece of wood on a faceplate. They should be a firm drive fit. Have a 13mm. (½in.) hole in the center of the wooden chuck, so that the work can be tapped out with a mallet and a piece of dowel when the job is finished. This system works well, but some precision is needed in recessing the chuck, since it is easy to make the hole too large. The process is one of trial and error, and if the fit is too slack some newspaper inside the chuck will take up the play.

If blanks are correctly fitted into such chucks the grip is quite surprising, and I have found

DESIGNS FOR THE HOME

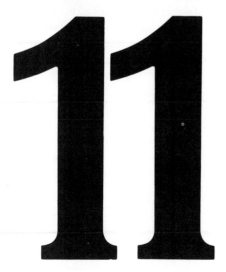
11

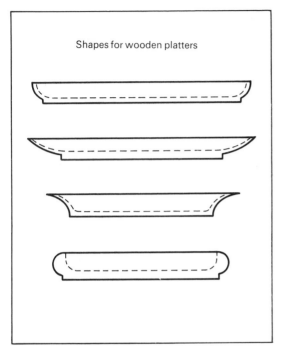

Shapes for wooden platters

Fig. 11-1

Fig. 11-2 An hourglass is a nice combination of spindle and faceplate work, calling for accuracy if the project is to be a success.

the system most helpful over the years. Its greatest disadvantage is that it takes quite some time to complete a project because of the fiddling involved in getting the chuck size correct.

In the making of plates, unless the turner is expert in the use of faceplate gouges, he will be best advised to use sharp scrapers, cutting lightly and to achieve his final finish through several coats of lacquer sealer, each one thoroughly sanded.

Hourglasses

Hourglasses are interesting projects, making a pleasant combination of spindle and screw chuck turning (Fig. 11-2). The glasses them-

selves are readily available through turnery equipment suppliers, in various colors of sand. They are not always exactly accurate to an hour, and I have found that odd ones seem to be inadequately sealed, so that the sand can sometimes become slightly damp, which causes occasional blockages. Normally they work well and are very popular as gifts.

The small spindles can test the skill of a beginner as regards his gouge and chisel work, but they should on no account be scraped to shape (Fig. 11-3).

The main thing to watch is exact measurement, for in a well-made example the three spindles will be identical in shape and

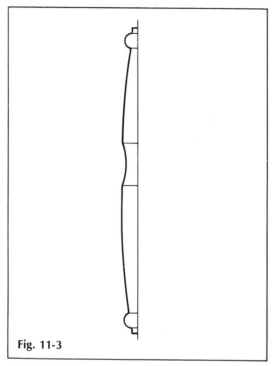

Fig. 11-3

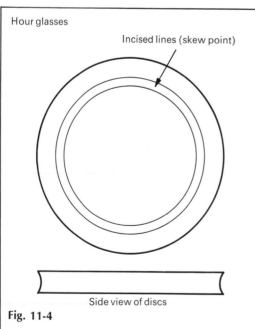

Hour glasses

Incised lines (skew point)

Side view of discs

Fig. 11-4

length. Their length depends on the size of glass used and the pins. They should be turned from three separate pieces of wood; any attempt to cut all three from one length at one mounting is likely to be unsuccessful because, at this sort of diameter, the wood will whip badly.

The wood used for each piece should be 25mm.–50mm. (1in.–2in.) longer than the spindle length, the waste at each end being sawn off afterwards. The discs for top and bottom can be made on a woodscrew chuck and are quite straightforward, (Fig. 11-4). The screw holes will be hidden by the hourglass when the job is assembled. I use the 9mm. (⅜in.) bowl gouge for this sort of operation, a little on its side, with light slicing cuts.

If the lathe has an indexing head, this can be used to locate the drilling points for the three holes which take the spindles. These are glued into place. The holes are spaced at 120° intervals. If there is no indexing head available, the marking will have to be done with the aid of a protractor.

Assembled with some strong adhesive, these decorative articles are quite robust. Egg-timer glasses can also be bought and these, although smaller, are made along similar lines.

Tripod Tables

The making of a tripod table, be it a tiny wine table or a larger and more general purpose version, is a most interesting and enjoyable operation (Fig. 11-5). The man who owns a bandsaw and perhaps a belt sander will be able to make quick work of the legs, and if the top is to be turned, this is exactly the same procedure as in making a circular tray. It can,

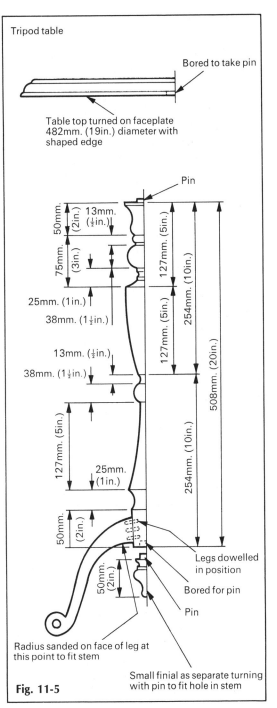

Tripod table

Bored to take pin

Table top turned on faceplate 482mm. (19in.) diameter with shaped edge

Pin

50mm. (2in.)
13mm. (½in.)
75mm. (3in.)
127mm. (5in.)
25mm. (1in.)
38mm. (1½in.)
13mm. (½in.)
38mm. (1½in.)
127mm. (5in.)
254mm. (10in.)
508mm. (20in.)
127mm. (5in.)
25mm. (1in.)
254mm. (10in.)
50mm. (2in.)

Legs dowelled in position

50mm. (2in.)
Bored for pin
Pin

Radius sanded on face of leg at this point to fit stem

Small finial as separate turning with pin to fit hole in stem

Fig. 11-5

of course, be made octagonal if preferred and perhaps carved or molded around the edges.

The square blank for the table pillar is quite a hefty lump of wood, and it might pay to drop the lathe speed a little. Most of my spindle work is done at about 2000 r.p.m., but for this a reduction to 1500 r.p.m. in the early stages might make things more comfortable. The larger the blank when working between centers, the more important it becomes to see that the material is mounted safely in the lathe, with the driving center sufficiently deep in the wood and the tailstock properly adjusted. This is another of those jobs where a tool rest which goes the full length of the machine will be an advantage.

As usual, the first operation is the roughing down from a square to a cylinder which will not take long with a sharp 50mm. (2in.) gouge, though with workpieces of this nature it may be advantageous to plane or saw off the corners first to reduce vibration. This mainly depends on how rigid the lathe is.

Having roughed the wood down to a cylinder, my next move is always to run a sharp skew along the top of it with a light cut to produce the smoothest finish possible, then to stop the lathe and examine the entire surface by touch and by eye for cracks. Internal cracks, known as shakes, are sometimes caused when a tree is felled. These may not be apparent when the wood is first put into the lathe, especially if the surface is straight from the saw. If they are discovered after all the careful work has been done, it is most disappointing.

Assuming all to be well, the wood will now be taken down along its full length to a diameter a fraction greater than the maximum required, then carefully marked out in pencil. This will do if only one table is to be produced, but if they are to be turned in quantity, some convenient form of marking device will be needed. The best answer is a strip of wood which has some brads driven in at the requisite positions, the heads of which are nipped off and points produced by filing. With care, it will be possible to lay this along the tool rest and press the points into the revolving wood, so ensuring accuracy. Make quite sure that the tool rest is really close to the work to prevent the strip of wood from slipping between the two.

Diameters are now set out by cutting in with a parting tool and measuring carefully with calipers, allowing a little extra thickness for final trimming. These parting tool cuts will help the shaping by separating the main features of the design. The continuation of the stem below the junction of legs and pillar can sometimes be a separate turning if the design makes this desirable. In such a case the main pillar will be bored at its bottom end before turning to take the pin on the other section.

It is as well to check the section where the legs are to be fitted, to make quite sure that it is straight, which can be done easily enough with a straight-edge. To facilitate a secure fixing of pillar to table top, a pin can be turned on the pillar and a separate disc made on a woodscrew chuck with a hole to take the pin. This disc is screwed and glued to the table top, the pillar subsequently being glued to it.

The turning of objects like the pillar of a tripod table should be done with great care; whereas a mistake in the making of an egg-cup or a small table lamp is a nuisance, such a mistake on a prime piece of material this size

can be very costly. Having gone to the trouble of marking the job out accurately, the mind must not be allowed to wander, because it is ridiculously easy to start a cut in entirely the wrong place!

There are various methods which can be used to effect the fixing of the legs to the pillar, including tenons and sliding dovetails, but with the marvelous adhesives now available, dowels are a quick and efficient answer. The legs obviously have to be set at 120° points around the pillar, and here again, the dividing head of the lathe can be used.

For those unfamiliar with this device, a few words of explanation may be helpful. Some Rockwell Delta lathes have a front pulley with twenty-four equally spaced holes drilled around its flange and a locking pin mounted in the headstock casting. Taking the job in hand as an example, the method of operation is quite simple. With the turned pillar set up in the lathe, the locking pin is pushed in to engage with one of the holes in the pulley. This holds the work steady in the lathe while a pencil line is scribed along it, using the tool rest as a guide. With the locking pin reset eight holes round the flange, another line is drawn, and the procedure is repeated to establish the third. These pencil marks are, of course, the dowel center lines.

Accuracy is essential throughout the whole process of fitting legs to these tables, and the dowel holes must be drilled radially to the pillar, or the results will be poor. The face of each leg where it meets the pillar must be made concave, since the face it is to meet is convex and the curvature must be exact. This is ensured by sanding the faces with a drum sander, which has a radius equal to that of the pillar where the legs are fitted. The drum sander is merely a piece of wood turned to correct diameter on a woodscrew chuck, slotted along one side, and wrapped in abrasive paper. The ends of the paper are pushed into the slot and secured by tapping in a strip of softwood. The sanding of these concave faces will be facilitated by setting up a platform or table which will allow the leg to be held correctly in relation to the drum. Considerable heat may be generated through friction in this job, so the wood should be sanded for a few seconds only at a time, with short breaks to allow it to cool. Use new abrasive paper, or the wood will burn.

Circular Picture Frames

These can be used for such items as small pictures, photographs, particularly unusual or attractive tiles, and even pot lids left over from Victorian days. A picture framer who came to me once for a short course in turning was most interested in these, because he said there was considerable demand for circular frames, which were not readily available through normal commercial channels. Picture frames of the sort described here can also be used to make decorative plaques from dried grasses and flowers, with a domed clock glass fitted to a wooden frame. The result can be most attractive.

The turning is not difficult, though it certainly calls for careful work and sharp edges, especially when cutting through with the parting tool to separate the frame proper from the blank. The wooden disc for the frame is cut out on a bandsaw and mounted on a woodscrew chuck. The edges are trimmed to a circle with a smooth surface, using a gouge rather than a scraper, and the width of the frame is marked with the point of a skew or a pencil. Since this is the front of the frame, the rabbet width is included.

The outer edge is shaped with the 9mm. (⅜in.) gouge, and a parting tool cut is made immediately to the right of the line which marks the frame width, going about half-way through the wood. At this stage the work is sealed with lacquer and sanded, this being repeated until the required quality of finish is achieved.

The partly completed blank is removed from the chuck and replaced by a larger piece of hard- or softwood which is then recessed with a parting tool to take the blank as a drive fit, the turned face going in first. To make sure that the waste center piece will not fly out when it is eventually separated, a screw can now be put through it into the homemade chuck—a proceeding which also boosts the morale of the beginner!

Carefully marking the overall width of the frame on the blank first, the rabbet must now be cut, again using a sharp parting tool. When the rabbet is completed, the center part can be separated by going right through with the parting tool and removed. After sealing and sanding, the frame is finished.

Rabbet sizes will vary according to the ultimate use of the frame, whether or not glass is to be used, and so on. If the frame is large enough and the rabbet sufficiently deep, a plywood disc can be fitted behind the picture and held in place by means of small brass tabs, screwed at one end to the frame. A plywood prop stand can be fitted with a piece of thread to prevent it from slipping outwards, and a coat or two of polyurethane will finish the job. Smaller frames can be backed with cardboard and sealed around the edge with brown gummed paper. For wall-mounted frames, small brass rings can be purchased, with screwed pins attached.

89

Most newcomers to woodturning will be their own first customers for these items which are relatively simple to make. Sheffield tool manufacturers will supply turning tools "blade only." The woodturner usually has his own definite ideas about the sort of handle he likes. My preference is for a length of about 355mm. (14in.), which provides a good leverage factor to help control incipient "digs."

My lathes now run mainly for the benefit of my students so the driving belts are kept slack, with just enough tension for normal work, so that a dig-in will stop the work without doing any damage. The man who has a habit of letting the tools dig into the work should certainly wear a face visor.

VARIOUS ITEMS

12

Most handle blanks can be cut from 38mm. (1½in.) square stock, about 50mm. (2in.) longer than the finished job is required to be. Ferrules are cut from off-cuts of copper or steel pipe; plumbers often have a supply. Length and diameter of these is not critical, but will vary according to size of tool.

Before turning up a tool handle the wood should be pre-drilled in the manner described earlier, to accommodate the tang, and the hole so produced will be placed at the tailstock end (Fig. 12-1A). The square of wood is mounted in the lathe and run down to a cylinder with a roughing gouge, which can also do most of the shaping in a job of this nature. At the right-hand end, a pin is cut with the parting tool, of a size to fit the ferrule. This need not be a really tight fit, since driving in the tang will tighten it (Fig. 12-1B).

At the desired distance from the driving center, a V-shaped cut is made with the point of a skew—cutting rather than scraping. Gouges are now employed to shape the

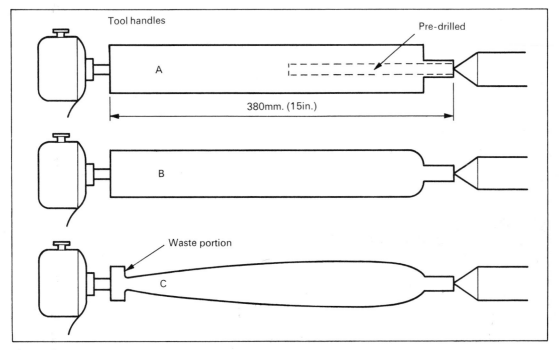

Fig. 12-1A—C

handle, and the surface can be smoothed with the skew chisel, taking a light cut and producing a shaving.

After the skew smoothing cut, the job can be sanded if necessary, the V-cut at the end is deepened to leave about 6mm. (¼in.) of wood, then the job is taken from the lathe and the waste nipped off with a saw (Fig. 12-1C). Two or three coats of polyurethane will give a good finish and any dense, straight-grained hardwood can be used for handles.

Pusher for Power Planers

Those who have a powered jointer machine should certainly have one of these useful little devices which may well prevent serious

injury; the one illustrated provides good exercise in the use of the 13mm. (½in.) spindle gouge.

The construction of the board itself is shown in Fig. 12-2, but it is important to let the small cross member into the wood rather than glue it straight on. The knobs are turned from small blocks on a 38mm. (1½in.) woodscrew chuck, and with care they could be made identical. Resist any temptation to scrape them, as they will be far better if properly cut.

Furniture Knobs

Knobs for furniture are turned on a woodscrew chuck and parted off when finished. They can be turned with a pin which is glued

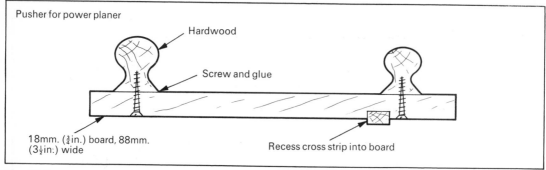

Pusher for power planer

Hardwood

Screw and glue

18mm. (¾in.) board, 88mm. (3½in.) wide

Recess cross strip into board

Fig. 12-2

Fig. 12-3 Planer pusher made in the workshop. Knobs are turned on a woodscrew chuck.

into a hole or left flat at the base and fixed with a screw. They are often from beech and stained as necessary. Fig. 12-4 shows a variety of designs.

Shovel handles are turned between centers.

Toys

I am quite unable to resist the inclusion of the old woodturning toys—the yo-yo, whip top, and skittles. These are simple to produce and make delightful presents.

Yo-Yo

The yo-yo can be made as illustrated in Fig. 12-5 by fixing a suitable piece of wood to the woodscrew chuck and turning it to a cylinder of the required diameter. The end is now rounded over to give the radius and its surface cleaned up with a gouge. The groove for the string is cut with a really sharp parting tool, skimming the cut if necessary to prevent the tool from overheating. This is just a matter of withdrawing the tool when it begins to bind and then going back in, widening the cut just a little.

The parting tool can now be used on the left of the job, partially separating it from the waste portion, and several cuts can be made, if desired, to give plenty of room for forming the radius with the gouge. Sand as well as possible, then continue the separation with the parting tool until only about 6mm. (¼in.) remains at the center. A sharp tenon saw or a hacksaw blade will finish the job.

If the parting tool is taken right to the center, as it could be, there is a danger of leaving a very rough spot, which cannot be put right by

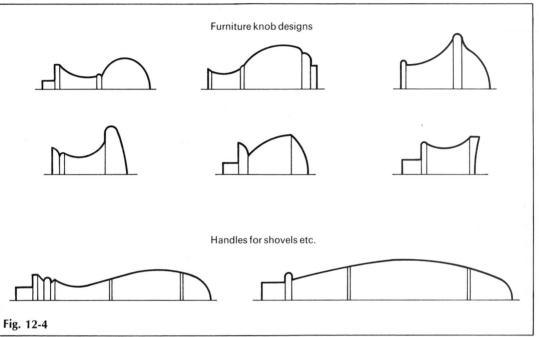

Furniture knob designs

Handles for shovels etc.

Fig. 12-4

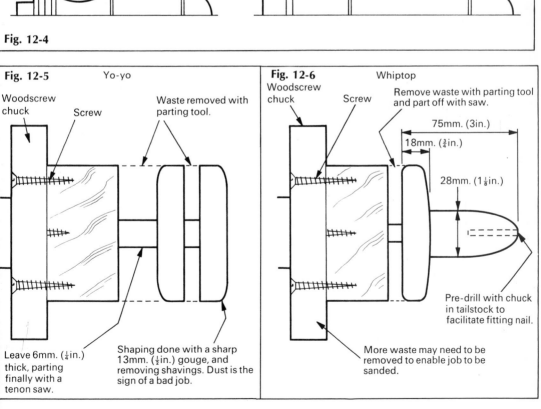

Fig. 12-5 Yo-yo

Woodscrew chuck

Screw

Waste removed with parting tool.

Leave 6mm. ($\frac{1}{4}$in.) thick, parting finally with a tenon saw.

Shaping done with a sharp 13mm. ($\frac{1}{2}$in.) gouge, and removing shavings. Dust is the sign of a bad job.

Fig. 12-6 Whiptop

Woodscrew chuck

Screw

Remove waste with parting tool and part off with saw.

75mm. (3in.)

18mm. ($\frac{3}{4}$in.)

28mm. (1$\frac{1}{8}$in.)

Pre-drill with chuck in tailstock to facilitate fitting nail.

More waste may need to be removed to enable job to be sanded.

sanding. Some good quality lead-free enamel paints will make the yo-yo look like professional work.

Whip Top

The top is an easy job, but it is still quite possible to make a mess of it if insufficient care is taken. A screw chuck alone can be used without the tailstock, but the latter can be brought up with very light pressure to steady the job.

Fig. 12-6 shows how the turning was done, and little more needs to be said. Before commencing the turning itself, it is a good idea to put a chuck in the tailstock with a 3mm. (⅛in.) drill and feed this some way into the revolving wood by means of the handwheel.

This hole will give some guidance for the screw or nail which is subsequently fitted and so prevent splitting.

Skittles

The skittles will provide scope for the imagination of the turner, both in respect of shape and final painting. They are fun to make and the construction of the wooden balls is a real test of skill which is very difficult indeed. From a practical viewpoint, a tennis ball would be better, being softer.

Such items can be turned individually between centers with a little waste at the head end, but they can, if preferred, be turned up in "sticks" of three or four at a time and parted later (Fig. 12-7).

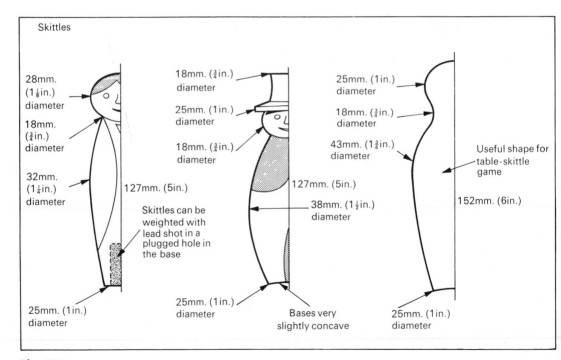

Fig. 12-7

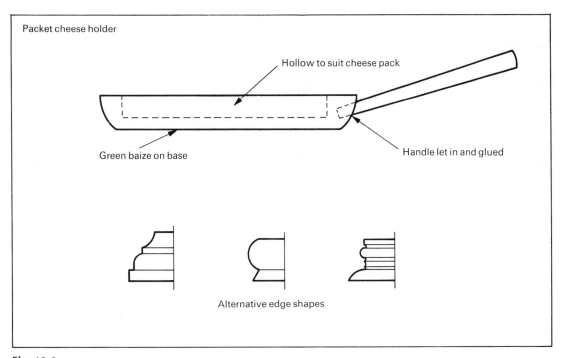

Fig. 12-8

Make sure that the paint used is lead-free and of good quality, or it will soon be chipped.

Packet Cheese Holder

Holders for packet cheeses (Fig. 12-8) are popular and very useful items and can be completed in about half an hour after some practice. The main body is turned on a screw chuck with three screws, shaping with the 9mm. (⅜in.) deep-fluted gouge, hollowing with a sharp parting tool, and *lightly* cleaning up the interior with a square-ended scraper.

Figs. 12-9 through 12-13 show the procedure. First a square of elm to be used for the packet cheese holder has diagonals drawn in to locate the center. A circle is then scribed with dividers before bandsawing the disc. If desired, the wood could first be passed over a jointer. Fig. 12-11 shows the turning in progress. Note the 9mm. (⅜in.) bowl gouge which was used to make a good job of the end grain. When turning is completed, after hollowing roughly with the parting tool, the recess is cleaned up with a scraper to receive the cheese packet. Drawing round the cheese packet with a pencil may help as a rough guide to the area to be hollowed.

The handle is turned between centers and glued into a hole in the body. The packet cheese which have a transparent lid look best in these holders.

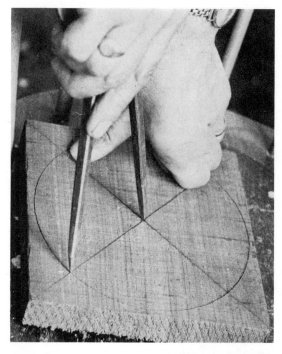

Fig. 12-9 Square of elm to be used for packet cheese holder has diagonals drawn in to locate center.

Fig. 12-10 Scribing circle with dividers before band-sawing the disc. If desired, wood could first be passed over a planer.

Fig. 12-11 The turning in progress. Note 9mm. (⅜ in.) bowl gouge, used to make a good job of the end grain.

Fig. 12-12 Cleaning up recess for cheese packet with scraper after hollowing roughly with parting tool.

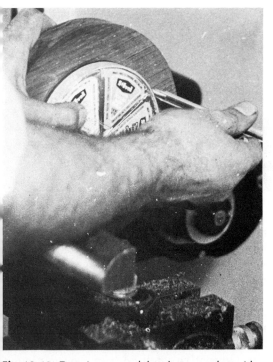

Fig. 12-13 Drawing around the cheese packet with a pencil may help as a rough guide to the area to be hollowed.

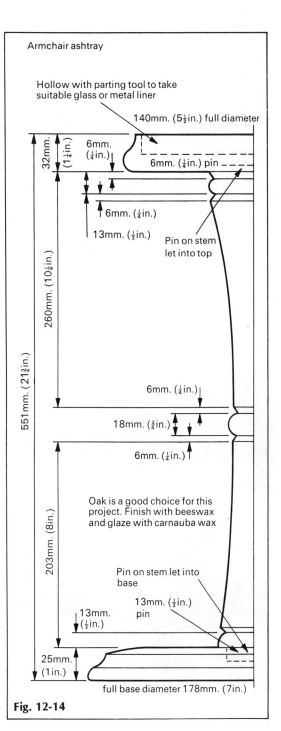

Armchair ashtray

Hollow with parting tool to take suitable glass or metal liner

140mm. (5½in.) full diameter

32mm. (1¼in.)

6mm. (¼in.)

6mm. (¼in.) pin

6mm. (¼in.)

13mm. (½in.)

Pin on stem let into top

260mm. (10¼in.)

551mm. (21¾in.)

6mm. (¼in.)

18mm. (¾in.)

6mm. (¼in.)

Oak is a good choice for this project. Finish with beeswax and glaze with carnauba wax

203mm. (8in.)

Pin on stem let into base

13mm. (½in.) pin

13mm. (½in.)

25mm. (1in.)

full base diameter 178mm. (7in.)

Fig. 12-14

Armchair Ashtray

Napkin Rings

The armchair ashtray, or smoker's companion as they are often called, is basically similar in its method of construction to a floor lamp and can be made with the stem in one piece or in two sections. If variations on the design are tried, stability should be a primary consideration as these things must obviously not fall over (Fig. 12-14). It is, of course, pointless to have an ashtray made entirely of wood, which will rapidly become charred, so a liner must be provided. This could be spun on the lathe from copper sheet, or a small pottery saucer could be used.

This is another fairly simple project in which the end product makes a welcome gift. However, there is a disadvantage in that the making of a set of these rings can take quite some time, especially if a stand is made for them. A few notes on the procedure may be helpful.

These rings can be made by turning a short piece of wood to a suitable size on a screw chuck, shaping the outside, hollowing with a sharp parting tool to a depth greater than the length of the ring, sanding and polishing, then parting off from the waste. Beginners

Fig. 12-15 Turning a tapered softwood mandrel to hold napkin ring blanks.

Fig. 12-16 Blank mounted on softwood mandrel for turning to shape. Sharp gouges and light cuts will be required.

may have trouble with this method, in that it can be difficult to control the parting tool sufficiently to ensure that no taper is produced inside the ring. This tool may also cause spelching (breaking away of the wood) as the cut is completed. Parting off with a very fine toothed saw can make a better job.

An alternative method can be employed which is certainly more suitable where large numbers of rings are to be made. This process involves cutting a number of square blocks of wood to a suitable size, then drilling these on the lathe or drill press with a large cutter.

When the interior has been attended to with the drill, the blocks are mounted individually in the lathe by taping them firmly on to a piece of wood which has been turned to a slight taper (Fig. 12-15 and 12-16). This is driven between centers and provides sufficient frictional grip to permit the turning of the blocks to shape with a sharp gouge (Figs. 12-17 and 12-18).

The outside, when completed, can be sanded and polished, and the block is removed from the homemade mandrel. When sufficient blocks have been prepared in this manner, the insides and ends will require final attention. This part of the job calls for a wooden

Fig. 12-19 Softwood or hardwood block on wood-screw has been hollowed to accept a tight push fit of the rings for sanding and polishing the inside. Paper packing can be used, if required.

Fig. 12-17 Outside of ring shaped and sanded, ready for sealing and polishing.

Fig. 12-18 Napkin ring in yew, ready for removal from mandrel for internal treatment.

chuck made from scrap wood and mounted on a large screw chuck. The scrap wood is turned to a cylinder and hollowed with the parting tool to accept the rings as a good push fit. If they are too large, some paper inside the hole will improve the situation (Fig. 12-19). With the ring held firmly in this way, a sharp scraper used very lightly will clean up the insides and ends ready for sanding and polishing.

If scrapers must be used, always sharpen them by cleaning off the old wire edge on the side of the grinding wheel, then grinding the bevel once all the way round with sparks showing on top of the tool. This gives an edge which will cut quite well and is robust enough to last for a reasonable time.

For a job like the one described here, where scraping is the only approach yet a clean cut is called for, I would ticket the edge in the same way as a cabinetmaker sharpens his scraper. This gives an excellent edge, though the tool will become blunt more quickly than when normally ground. Ticketing is done by grinding the bevel, oilstoning the top surface to remove the burr, and then bending the edge forward by pressure from a hardened steel rod or the back of a gouge.

The construction of a stand for a set of these rings will present no problems. The turning is very similar to the making of a small table lamp.

Containers with Lids

Boxes and other containers with lids can be turned for a wide variety of purposes in all kinds of shapes. Small boxes made simply as ornaments from exotic timbers or built-up blanks can be interesting and attractive. Cig-

arette boxes, tobacco jars, cookie jars, and so forth are constantly in demand, particularly the well-made examples. (See chapter 5.)

The turning in this sort of work must be done with the greatest care, and all edges, whether those of cutting tools or scrapers, must be kept razor sharp by frequent sharpening.

The interiors of this type of construction will have to be scraped because they are deep in relation to the width, and it is not possible to keep the bevel of a gouge rubbing.

The hollowing can, in many cases, be helped by first boring a hole as large as possible and to a depth slightly less than that required for

Fig. 12-20 Use of template former to reproduce both female and male outlines.

the container. This can be widened as necessary with a parting tool or a square-ended scraper, and any interior curvature required can be produced with a round-nosed one.

The part of the turning which requires great accuracy and precise work is the forming of the matching rabbets on container and lid. Remember that further cuts can always be made and more wood removed, but it is not possible to put a shaving back once it has been cut off. In matching these rabbets, therefore, it will be necessary to stop the lathe at frequent intervals so that progress can be checked. If any doubt exists as to whether or not the wood is fully seasoned, the fit of a lid should be made a trifle slack to compensate for possible shrinkage.

Liners, and indeed handles for items such as cookie jars, can be obtained from turnery supply dealers, though they are becoming rather expensive.

Table Lighters

The production of a cigarette lighter for table use is not by any means difficult, and the lighter units themselves are readily available. Certain forms of built-up blank make particularly interesting lighters, which are decorative as well as useful.

This is a job for the screw chuck, requiring the use of three screws, and it is imperative that the blank be accurately centered if it is of the built-up variety. The lighter units normally fit into small cup-like containers which are recessed into the wood and secured with strong adhesive. A piece of green baize on the base will finish the job off quite well.

Fig. 12-20 illustrates a template former which some workers like to use for such jobs. It consists of a number of thin steel rods held by friction in a central bar. When pressed against a shape they reproduce both male and female outlines.

Before considering built-up turning in hardwood, which is a fascinating business, something should really be said about the building up of turning blanks from softwood or indeed from off-cuts of softwood (Fig. 13-1). The cost of timber is a major problem for most woodturners now, be they amateur or professional, and this is one way in which very attractive items can be made up at a low cost. This sort of work has the advantage of being relatively cheap to produce. The reason for this is in part the current popularity of pine furniture allied to the fact that there is not a great amount of turned softwood in the shops.

The inexperienced person will soon discover why the shops are so bare of turned softwood items, the reason being that such turning calls for rather skilled craftsmanship. It is often said that softwood cannot be turned, which is untrue, but it certainly cannot be

SOFTWOOD TURNINGS

Fig. 13-1 Built-up table lamp ready to have its wire and bulb holder fitted.

turned unless proper cutting techniques are used. When cut correctly and well finished, the grain can be very attractive. However, there is one problem with this material in that it is most unstable, being inclined to twist and warp at the slightest provocation and, indeed, to split. Large pieces of softwood are prone to this, but the built-up blank described here has considerable stability, because wherever possible the grain is alternated in adjacent pieces so that one pulls against another and cancels out the movement.

Softwood is light in color and looks very well if coated with clear varnish, but the temptation to stain it to resemble some other wood should be resisted. It can be tried, but it is difficult to achieve an even coloring due to the stain being soaked up rapidly by the end grain which becomes much darker than the rest of the surface.

Squares or pieces of 50mm. × 25mm. (2in. × 1in.) timber can be laminated to form blanks which are ready to be turned into bowls or dishes. If thicker blanks are required, two or more of these can be glued together, remembering to alternate the grain. Marked out with a pair of dividers and cut to a disc on the bandsaw, these will make very good bowls.

The adhesive should be given some thought. White Polyvinyl acetate glues as used in ordinary woodwork can be employed, but I have found that they permit some movement of the wood, and after a while the joints can be felt in the finished turning. A glue such as Secur-It or Tight Bond or Boat Armor Epoxy Resin which sets very hard will avoid this trouble. One does hear complaints that certain types of glue tend to take the edges off the turning tools rather quickly; indeed, this contains an element of truth, but it is the sort of complaint voiced by those who find the sharpening of tools a bother. In fact, putting a fresh edge on a gouge with the grindstone is a matter of a few seconds work.

It is also said, again wrongly, that small pieces of softwood cannot be turned on woodscrew chucks because either the screw will not hold or the wood slips round on the chuck. The former problem can be dealt with by using a longer and fatter screw than would be needed for hardwood, the latter by folding a piece of abrasive paper and putting it between the chuck and the wood. If the tools are sharp and the cuts light, all will be well.

If a blank is to be built up from squares, about 25mm.–38mm. (1in.–1½in.), it is very important to see that these are truly square, or there will be gaps everywhere in the assembled blank. This can be done by hand, by those with the time and skill, but use of the small planer ensures accuracy for the worker in a hurry. A fair batch of wood is prepared, two adjacent sides of each strip being planed smooth and at 90°, the remaining two cut with the thicknessing attachment, so that not only are the corners exactly 90°, but the thickness of the strips is the same each way.

The procedure is illustrated in Fig. 13-2 to 13-5. Timber is fed through a thicknessing attachment in preparation for cutting to make built-up assemblies. Fig. 13-3 shows completion of the thicknessing process. Wood is being pulled through from the rear of the machine. The feed rate should be steady, or a rippled surface will result. The thicknesser (Fig. 13-4) shows an adjustable plate with springs beneath it to hold wood against the plate as it is cut. Fig. 13-5 is an end-on view of the timber passing through the jointer thicknesser. The attachment also helps to protect the fingers.

Fig. 13-2 Feeding timber through a jointer, using thicknessing attachment in preparation for cutting to make built-up assemblies.

Fig. 13-3 Completed thicknessing process. Wood is being pulled through from rear of machine.

Fig. 13-4 Thicknesser showing adjustable plate with springs beneath it to hold wood against plate as it is cut.

Fig. 13-5 End view of timber passing through the planer-thicknesser.

When the blanks have been built up, pressure should be applied at room temperature for twenty-four hours to make quite sure that they are well and truly stuck. Never be tempted into turning a blank which has not been assembled for at least this period of time, preferably longer, or it may fly apart in the lathe and cause serious injury.

If the assembly of blanks with prepared material is carried out on a flat surface, the surface of the finished blanks should also be flat, but this does not always work out. The assembly may need to be run over a planer, especially if two are to be glued together.

Softwood can be used as described earlier to make up hollow blanks from strip material or, for vases and such like, squares can be glued together lengthwise to make up a square block which will have to be hollowed on the lathe. A woodscrew chuck with three screws will hold such blanks, if the screws are suitable, and light tailstock support can be given during the roughing down.

A gouge cannot be used for hollowing articles of this nature so a scraper is an unfortunate necessity, but if it is sharp and only light cuts are taken, it will do the job. After the hollowing, a wooden plug can be fitted in the end and the tailstock brought back while the job is finished off, sanded, and polished.

There is no magic method of making a rough piece of wood look as though it has been properly turned. The only thing which will make a finished turning look professional is the use of correct, professional methods with sharp tools, so the remarks here concerning various finishing materials assume that the object being polished has been well turned.

Abrasive paper should be in grades of medium down to fine or extra fine. Anything coarser than this will be more trouble than it is worth, because it will put deep scratches into the wood, and these are very difficult to take out.

Very fine steel wool can be used after sanding, the grade being 000 (Treble 0). Keep this steel wool away from the driving and tailstock centers, or it may suddenly wrap itself round them, which is not particularly dangerous, but rather disconcerting.

Beeswax constitutes a good filler. Apply it to the wood in an even coat, then melt it into the surface by a hard pressure with a pad of rag. Some optimists believe that if sandpaper is used instead of rag, a mixture of wood dust and wax will be driven into the surface of the work, thus making a better filler. If this is tried it will be found ineffective, as the abrasive paper instantly becomes clogged up by the wax. (In some ways cobbler's wax is preferable to beeswax, because it is harder and seems to bring up a better shine, but a reliable source of supply is hard to locate.)

Some eye protection is a good thing when doing this, as the wax gets very hot, and small particles going into the eyes can be very painful. Remember, too, that protection for the eyes in turning and grinding is important. Goggles or an eyeshield ought to be worn, though I make do with my spectacles. The amount of sanding done by a good turner is hardly sufficient to require the use of a face

FINISHING

14

mask, but I do use one of these when running a belt or disc sander.

Beeswax alone is not much good as a polish, but mixed with carnauba wax, one part carnauba to two of beeswax with a little turpentine, it does make a good polish. Carnauba, itself very hard, has the ability to harden other waxes. This mixture is applied to the wood in the same way as straight beeswax, but the amount of pressure required to polish it will be considerably less.

Carnauba wax used alone is tricky, and a fair amount of practice will be needed before the knack is acquired. Too little pressure gives it a whitish appearance and too much will melt it, bringing it up into dirty rings. Once properly done, however, the finish with this will be a beautiful gloss. It is not really good for articles which are likely to be handled a great deal because it soon begins to look grubby.

One substance which I use frequently is lacquer sealer, which is clear cellulose mixed with French chalk, in equal proportions by volume. This is applied to the wood while it is stationary, allowed to dry, then sanded thoroughly. Several coats may be needed and a lot of my turning has just a sealer finish with ordinary household furniture polish over the top.

Polyurethane is not used a great deal in turning, perhaps because it requires a certain amount of time to dry. The real trouble is that it cannot be used in the same room as the turning is done, because of the dust.

GLOSSARY OF TECHNIQUES AND EQUIPMENT

Cutting a Bead

Initial stages of roughing down a cylinder for practice in bead cutting.

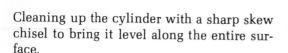

Cleaning up the cylinder with a sharp skew chisel to bring it level along the entire surface.

Preparation for bead cutting. Width has been marked lightly with point of skew chisel. These marks should not be made deep, or the chisel point will be overheated, and the wood will break away in front of the point, causing the tool to slip.

Correct position of chisel to begin left-hand half of bead. Cutting edge is parallel to axis of wood, right-hand side of tool clear of tool rest, height of chisel point above tool rest is correct.

In trimming the wood on each side of the bead only the point of the tool can be used, since it alone is receiving support from the tool rest.

The cutting of beads begins a little to each side of center, to avoid a sharp peak being formed.

Waste wood at sides of beads being cut away with skew chisel. The point only does the job, the rest of the blade is kept clear of the wood.

Multiple Beading

Spacing the beads by marking the revolving wood with a pair of dividers.

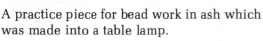

A practice piece for bead work in ash which was made into a table lamp.

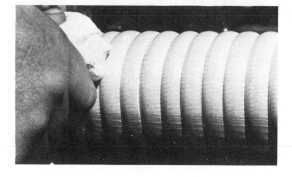

Close-up of matching beads used to make table lamp. Work of this nature with beads or coves which must be identical will improve the turner's ability at a surprising rate. Here friction polish is being applied after sanding sealer.

Polish enhances the beauty of the wood grain and imparts a good shine.

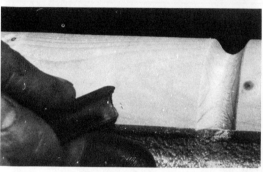

Cutting a Cove

A cove, right, is the opposite of a bead and the gouge is shown here in position to start cutting the left-hand half.

Cutting left-hand half of cove in softwood. Note how the gouge has rolled on to its back, the handle being lowered at the same time.

Gouges should be kept really sharp. The effect of a blunt one on softwood can be seen plainly here.

111

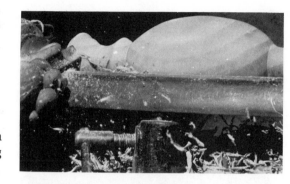

Forming a cove in base of a table lamp stem with a 13mm. (½in.) gouge. Very satisfying shavings will come from a really sharp tool.

Note that the gouge must cut downhill. If an uphill cut is attempted, as here, the part of the edge which is cutting will become unsupported as the gouge rolls (indicated by the pencil), and there will be a dig-in.

A rough line sometimes shows at the center of a cove, particularly on softwood, because at this point the cutting edge has no slicing action, crossing the grain at right angles.

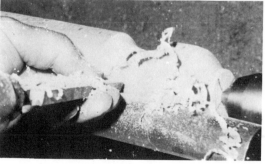

Here a scraper is being used—though normally a gouge would be employed—to cut a hollow in a piece of beech. Note that a properly sharpened scraper produces a shaving.

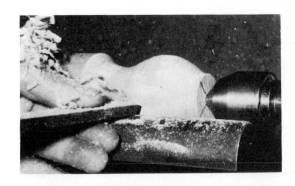

Although the scraper in use here is giving a shaving there is plenty of dust, and the surface finish is poor.

An 18mm. (¾in.) gouge produces even better shavings, but needs more skill in handling than the 13mm. (½in.) version.

Cutting a Curve

Rolling a skew chisel round a curve. This is an advanced cut and is difficult for a beginner. The shaving must leave the cutting edge in the area immediately adjacent to the short corner.

Forming a curve is easier with the gouge than with the chisel, but care must be taken to see that the supported part of the edge only is allowed to contact the wood. In this case it is the part between the center and the right-hand corner. Use of the center, or nose, should be avoided.

Grinding

152mm. (6in.) and 204mm. (8in.) double-ended grinders are precision made and extremely useful tools. The plastic guards should be used, but some form of eye shield should also be worn.

Grinding a skew chisel. The adjustable rests can be used, but I find the method shown to be far easier. The tool is moved slowly from side to side so that all the bevel is ground. Do not exert any pressure.

First stage in sharpening a scraper is the removal of the old burr or wire edge.

The scraper bevel is ground slowly, once round the entire edge, with sparks showing on top of the tool.

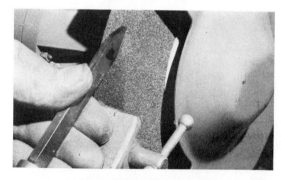

A parting tool must be ground lightly, starting at the heel and working to the edge by drawing the tool downwards.

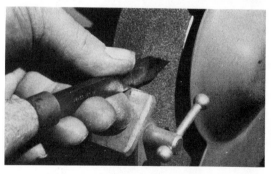

The sides of a parting tool need occasional treatment on the grinder to ensure that the cutting edge is wider than the metal behind it.

How the curvature of the wheel is reproduced on the bevel of the tool.

If a tool is held too high during grinding, as here, the bevel will be shortened and will become useless after a time. A lengthy grinding process is then needed to reshape the tool correctly.

Tools and Machines

This type of cutter is very useful for large holes which are not deep. It must be kept sharp and run at about 500 r.p.m.

With the headstock swivelled at 90 degrees to the lathe bed, drilling can be done by pushing the work on to the auger, but practice will be needed to keep the hole running straight.

The sander-grinder is a robust and extremely useful unit, with its 1 HP motor. In the foreground is the grindstone and disc sander with tilting table. At the back, right, is the hefty belt sander with adjustable fence.

The headstock of a lathe is very important. It must be very robust, with an easily adjustable bearing.

This lathe has an indexing head. The black-headed plunger just right of center is not, as many owners imagine, to lock the spindle to facilitate removal of faceplates, but to enable work to be divided around its circumference for fluting or drilling.

INDEX